IMPERFECT
PARENTING

Honest Stories from Global Parents

ADVANCE PRAISE

"Thank you for normalizing how disruptive and discombobulating it can be returning/combining work with parenting, particularly post-pandemic."

—*Vicki Broadbent*
Award-winning filmmaker, TV broadcaster, and author, *Mumboss: The Honest Mum's Guide To Surviving and Thriving at Work and at Home*

***

"There is such value and importance in sharing our stories. In parenthood, we are so often isolated within our thoughts and worries about being 'good enough', questioning our judgment, and attempting to manage some sort of balance within apparent societal expectations. But when we listen to the stories of others we are empowered to consider and validate our own. *Imperfect Parenting: Honest Stories from Global Parents* does just that. It acknowledges the complexities of parenthood so that we can lean into this incredible career and own it. This is the hopeful and encouraging read we need as parents in a post-pandemic era."

—*Geraldine Walsh*
Journalist and author, *Unraveling Motherhood: Understanding Your Experience Through Self-Reflection, Self-Care & Authenticity*

***

"In a world filled with countless parenting guides and manuals, this book stands apart. It is not a typical how-to guide; it is a raw and authentic collection of experiences shared by parents who have walked the path of raising their children. As I delved into the pages, I was struck by the honesty and vulnerability in each story.

What makes this book unique is the inclusion of perspectives from both fathers and mothers. It offers a diverse range of narratives that can be appreciated by readers of any gender. The co-authors, many of whom are professionals in behavioral science, bring their expertise to the table while acknowledging the challenges and uncertainties they faced in parenting.

This book is an invitation to connect, find solace in shared experiences, and grow as parents. I recommend it wholeheartedly to anyone seeking insights, guidance, and reassurance on their own parenting journey. Prepare to be moved, inspired, and empowered as you turn each page."

—*Sangeetha Parthasarathy*
Coach, speaker, and consultant, "Sangparth"

***

"One of the most powerful aspects of *Imperfect Parenting: Honest Stories from Global Parents* is its ability to address the unique needs and vulnerabilities of our children in this rapidly evolving society. But equally as important, is how it covers our relationships, as parents, in supporting our children and ourselves through these challenging times. The book is a testament to the power of community and connection. I came away reminded that, despite the difficulties we face, we can find strength in sharing our experiences and learning from one another."

—*Liam Preston, BEM*
Communications director and host,
Dad Still Standing podcast

***

"I am happy to recommend the book *Imperfect Parenting: Honest Stories from Global Parents* which is being co-authored by Aarthi Prabhakaran. Aarthi is a multifaceted person who loves to combine research with experiential wisdom. It is an insightful book providing practical tips for parents in today's challenging world. Her expertise along with her reflective approach will equip parents to nurture their child's unique individuality. Her keen understanding of the shifting cultural norms of society will provide valuable guidance to parents.

Here is wishing Aarthi Prabhakaran and her co-authors success and happiness in this endeavor."

—*Swapna Nair*
Teacher, counseling psychologist, and soft skills trainer

***

"As a budding pediatrician, I am thrilled to see a book like this being written and published. Parenting is a challenging journey, and having access to resources like this can make all the difference in supporting our children's growth and development. I am particularly excited to see a chapter focused on supporting LGBTQ+ children when they come out to their parents. It is essential that parents create a safe and accepting environment for their children, and this chapter provides valuable insights and advice on how to do so. I applaud you and the other authors for tackling this important topic and providing valuable insights on how to support these children. I look forward to reading and recommending this book and using it as a resource in my practice."

—*Dr. Chhavi Rosha*
Paediatrics and neonatology resident, Bharati Vidyapeeth

Jayne Ruff

Aarthi Prabhakaran

Anjna Parameswaran

Jaita Mullick

Chandrika Iyer

Jenna Clancey

Yagya Mahadevan

Denise Varughese

Ramakrishnan Rajamani

Preetha Bhaskar

Anuradha Gupta

Arren Williams

First Printing: 2023

Hardcover ISBN: 978-81-958695-8-9
Paperback ISBN: 978-81-958695-9-6

Cover design by Manoj Vijayan
Typeset by Manoj Gupta
Edited by Jyotirmoy Chaudhuri
Print by Repro India Limited

Disclaimer: All views and claims expressed in this book are solely those of the authors and do not necessarily represent those of their affiliated organizations, or those of the publisher, the editors and the reviewers.

LetsAuthor
www.letsauthor.com

CONTENTS

ACKNOWLEDGMENTS

Jayne Ruff and Aarthi Prabhakaran

The coming together of 12 global authors to produce this book has been accompanied by an incredible level of support, guidance, and endorsement from many people across the world. Aarthi and I, as lead authors, would like to take a moment to recognize and thank them.

We give our heartfelt thanks to the LetsAuthor team for conceiving the idea of a book on parenting in today's chaotic and ever-changing world. We are deeply grateful for the opportunity to share our stories in the hope that they offer comfort and connection to many other parents across the world today. Thank you to LetsAuthor founder, Dr. Saumita Banerjee, for her unwavering belief in the book and encouragement throughout its development. You have patiently navigated us through our first authoring experience and kept us on track at each step of the writing journey.

Thank you to each of our co-authors and their respective families and wider support networks. We have grown from our starting point as strangers into a devoted team with shared aspirations. It has been an absolute honour and privilege to get to know and work with each of you, and we have learned so much from reading your words. We thank you for your time and effort, and for your openness and honesty in sharing your personal experiences for the greater good. This collective passion, energy, and desire to make a positive difference in the lives of parents and children today is what makes this book so special.

A special thanks to Mina Dilip and Arthy Sriram who took time amidst their busy schedules to provide such thoughtful forewords to our book. We are so very appreciative of this. We are also exceptionally humbled by the endorsements shared for this book by a group of inspirational professionals whom we greatly admire and respect.

We would also like to thank all the people who supported the birth of the book through our crowdfunding campaign, both financially and by sharing far and wide with friends and contacts. Your faith and confidence in our book have been a constant motivator to all involved in its creation.

Aarthi and I would like to thank our husbands for championing us to keep on going with the book whilst balancing our busy work, study and home lives, and for always being by our sides as equal partners through the highs and lows of parenting.

Finally, we would like to thank our children. You have taught us more about ourselves than we could ever explain in one book, and it is this growth that makes parenting so wonderfully powerful. Thank you; we love you dearly.

FOREWORD

In recent years, parenting has emerged as a hot topic of discussion in various circles. A couple of generations ago, parenting was not a much-talked-about subject. Traditionally, several Eastern cultures took parenting in their stride, often normalizing certain parenting decisions and behaviors which have come into question today. In fact, in many Asian cultures, people barely paid attention to concepts like co-regulation, reinforcement, or behavior shaping. Spanking children when they misbehaved was the norm, and many of today's parents themselves grew up with parents who thought it was perfectly acceptable to hit, smack or publicly scold their children.

Today, things are very different. There is a lot more awareness among parents about the ill effects of abuse in any form, a greater willingness to learn and follow best practices, and an improvement in parent-child relationships all over the world. As a child psychotherapist, I end up working more with parents than with children on most days. This is because children in therapy often turn out to be "index clients," which means their behavior issues are a mere reflection of ineffective parenting practices. Working with parents, and guiding them in communicating effectively with their children, helps educate them about the importance of offering unconditional acceptance and support, which is what all children need. Having said that, it is important to acknowledge that along with professional support, tips, and guidance, every parent also seeks assurance, acceptance, and comfort.

Imperfect Parenting: Honest Stories from Global Parents is an ideal resource for those who are seeking the comfort of knowing that they are not alone in parenting children through difficult and challenging circumstances, fraught with change and uncertainty. This book contains honest, down-to-earth accounts of parenting experiences written by a dozen different authors from all over the world. It offers irrefutable evidence to support the fact that some parenting challenges are universal. In this highly relatable and heart-warming collection of personal stories that explore the ups and downs of being around children, you will find yourself nodding, smiling, or musing intensely as you read through the personal experiences, challenges, and strategies adopted by different parents under trying circumstances.

Packed with practical tips on managing change and ambiguity, *Imperfect Parenting: Honest Stories from Global Parents* can help you open your mind to newer ways of thinking about parenting and childcare. As you read the diverse stories written by this cross-cultural variety of authors, you will also notice that there is no one-size-fits-all approach to parenting. Every child is unique and different; so is every parent. And it is this uniqueness and diversity that help bridge the gap between feeling lost, frustrated, or anxious, and feeling calm, stable, and reassured about parenting.

One of the greatest strengths of a parent is fostering a good relationship with children while staying connected to a larger community of parents, to share stories, advice, tips, experiences, and even woes! It is indeed truly comforting to know that we are not alone in this and that parents all over the world are battling the same challenges as we are. This book is sure to guide, reassure and comfort you as you navigate the complex journey of parenting, which can be exciting, rewarding, and enjoyable as well as scary, uncertain, and challenging. Enjoy each story and notice how much you are able to identify with each author.

—*Mina Dilip*
Play Therapist (certified by Leeds Beckett University, UK)
Sand Tray Therapist (accredited by the Sand Tray Training Institute of New Mexico, USA)

Parenting is a unique experience and a journey to be enjoyed. In this beautiful journey, as a mother of two grown-up children and with my experience as a Counseling Psychologist working as a School Counselor, I have learned a lot from children and parents.

Every parent wishes to be the best parent and empower their children with the best of their resources. Raising a child is anything but easy. Children look at parents as their first role models. Parents are the greatest teachers of their children and can help them to overcome tough situations, supporting and nurturing them to become more mentally strong. Yet, there is no perfect way of parenting; no right or wrong approach to raising children. Mistakes are opportunities to learn, and this holds true for parenting too. In this book, each one of the global parents as authors share their own valuable lessons from their journey of mindful parenting, the challenges and happy moments, and the nuances of parenting based on their experiences, which will be a very useful and most likely relatable read for all parents.

Parenting is a rapturous experience. In this changing world, raising children while balancing between personal and professional life is an everyday challenge for most parents. It is not easy to be a parent juggling between home and work. With the constant pressure on both ends, it takes a toll on the physical and emotional well-being of the parents. Understanding and practicing varied strategies is shared by an author in one of the chapters of the book.

Everything starts from within. This is beautifully explained in one of the chapters of the book. It is essential and helpful when parents reflect on themselves and heal their own self before turning to their parenting roles. Parents might have had challenges during their childhood years and processing and healing them will help them to handle their emotions during parenting.

All parents go through a plethora of emotions as an individual and as a parent. One of the authors honestly discusses the importance of being compassionate with ourselves while raising our children. Parental self-compassion and self-care have a strong influence on child development. Nurturing yourself will help in bringing up more thriving kids. Being compassionate and gentle parents helps us understand and nurture our children much better.

Parents have a huge responsibility in guiding children to become much stronger not only physically but more importantly mentally. With the technology boom in all facets of our life, parents often feel that parenting has become more difficult in this modern age. Technology has its own advantages and disadvantages. Digital mindfulness is a skill to be practiced by modern parents in the healthy upbringing of their children. With the shared experiences of one author on parenting in the digital age, readers will find meaningful insights about how they can use technology wisely as parents and also teach their children positive practices.

Gender sensitivity begins at home. If you really want your child to be gender-sensitive, you need to be the role model they can follow. When children have questions or concerns related to their gender expression or sexual orientation, parents need to understand and support them to be feel accepted at home and by society. Give them the space to explore and connect with their gender and sexual identity in a meaningful way. This book has chapters that share insightful experiences of parents navigating gender sensitivity, gender expression and sexual orientation.

Single parents handle multiple responsibilities in bringing up their children. Parents become single for varied reasons, and they face several additional challenges than parents who together raise their children. Likewise, parents of children with health conditions often encounter added pressures at home and within wider society. These honest experiences about single parenting and raising a child with special needs are shared by two authors in the book.

There is nothing like learning from one another's true-life experiences for a better tomorrow. Connecting with these stories helps us to empathize, and consequently develop and evolve our own parenting strategies so we can grow along with our children. The readers of this book will gain immense, thoughtful, and insightful inputs into raising children in this modern world.

—Arthy Sriram
Counseling Psychologist
ACA Certified Professional Supervisor

INTRODUCTION

Jayne Ruff

"No parent is ALWAYS conscious, gentle, positive, peaceful and authentic. We have to CHOOSE to be and practice moment by moment… day after day. The more we practice, the stronger we grow."

—Leila Schott

WHAT CAN I EXPECT FROM THIS BOOK?

This is not a "how to" guide. There are no "five steps," "models," "frameworks," or "top tips." If you are looking for answers on the right way and wrong way to parent, then this book may not be for you (although we strongly believe that with an open mind, everyone can take something from it).

What this book offers is a collection of real-life stories written by mothers and fathers from across the globe, who have come together to express openly, honestly, and vulnerably the highs and lows of their parenting journeys and what they have learned along the way.

We share perspectives from the early parenting years, life with teenage kids, and the transition to becoming a grandparent. We talk not just about what we have done (and not done), but how it has felt. This raw emotion is often missing from more traditional parenting books and yet is at the heart of what makes parenting both incredibly rewarding and endlessly challenging.

Every story explores a topic that is personal to the author, and that we also know is experienced by many parents across the world today; balancing work and home life, raising a child as a single parent, empowering our children in a digital world, and re-parenting and re-educating ourselves while raising a family.

As there is no one-size-fits-all approach to parenthood, each story offers an individual take on a core parenting theme. Some chapter themes may be more relevant to your personal journey, and the stage of parenting you are at, than others. My co-authors and I invite you to join us all on our unique parenting journeys in the hope that we can offer you a richness of perspectives to connect with in small or sizable ways.

WHY DO I NEED THIS BOOK NOW?

The years 2020 and 2021 have gone down in history as two of the toughest years for the whole world in recent memory. The global pandemic impacted every generation; baby boomers, Gen X, millennials, and Gen Z were all affected in both common and specific ways. Climate change is accelerating. There is war, civil unrest, and financial recessions. Advances in technology have brought with them the good, the bad, and the ugly. The frequency and speed of change today can be overwhelming.

As parents, we are no strangers to change, although we might not always see it this way. There is arguably no bigger personal change than becoming a parent. It is a transformation that is often accompanied by a plethora of different emotions; from ecstasy to overwhelm and everything in between. How we see ourselves internally and how we view our place in the world shifts, influencing our thinking and behaviors across every area of our life into the future. Add into this mix the fact that we are living in an ever-evolving and often uncertain world and it becomes abundantly clear why understanding and appreciating how we, and our children, experience change is vital to our growth as a parent and a person today.

We are living in a time where we must deal with change almost every second. To keep up with ever-changing times, it has become a necessity to keep ourselves in tandem with what is changing, by learning to adapt on the go. What was familiar to each of us growing up has evolved at a rate that far outpaces the changes of generations before us. Gone are the days when a single educational degree qualification was enough to sustain a career spanning many decades. Each career chapter we turn to requires that we stay on top of new developments and embrace the opportunity to continuously learn and grow. Parenting is no different (and yes, we view parenting as a rewarding career, albeit a lifelong one, with evolving roles and responsibilities).

When it comes to raising children, the rise of social media and digital living has seen our dictionary of parenting terms expand exponentially. This has its pros and cons. I remember my mother flicking through the pages of her well-used "childhood illnesses" manual every time my brother and I were sick; the pages curled at the edges from hot fingers frantically searching for guidance on how best to treat the latest skin rash or vomiting bug. Today, a quick Google search gives me all the answers I need in seconds— and more (not always helpful!). I gained instant reassurance from my early morning WhatsApp messaging with other first-time parents in those first few weeks at home with a new baby, and I have also felt the negative impact of information overload and unhelpful comparison to others online.

As a psychologist specializing in change, I am very aware of both the challenges and opportunities navigating any change can bring. The whirring thoughts, feelings, and emotions that often accompany a change of any type can get in the way of paving a meaningful route through it. With different areas of our lives more intertwined than ever before, it can be hard to step back and see the best way forward. This is an emotional support book for parents raising kids in times of unprecedented change and uncertainty, in an evolving world that's fast-paced, unpredictable, ambiguous, and often different from our experienced childhoods, for better or worse.

HOW WILL THESE STORIES HELP ME AS A PARENT?

Communication sits at the heart of successful change, and storytelling is a powerful tool to help people engage with and take positive action through it. Humans have been telling stories for tens of thousands of years, which means our brains are hardwired to engage with the narratives we read and hear. Stories are authentic human experiences, which we have relied on since the Paleolithic period to help us make sense of the unknowns around us.

While the modern world offers unlimited access to huge quantities of information and data, I believe that one of the biggest blockers to reaping the benefits of this insight is the fact that the way it is presented—and how we tend to engage with it—is decontextualized. Our brains then process this information, and our related behavior, as either right or wrong. And so, I believe that it is not that we have too much information, rather we have not yet developed the strategies we need to constructively process and make choices about how we best use it.

Through storytelling, this book aims to bring back connection. To create a sense of community, united through the many shared emotions parenthood sparks: excitement, worry, pride, and guilt to name just a few. To encourage more parents to confidently speak up about the positives and the challenges of parenthood, however we experience these.

This book does not teach, tell or dictate any particular parenting style or approach. Its purpose is simple: to share the different changes each parent has navigated and the choices they have made in an open and non-judgmental way, in the hope that these unfiltered stories offer reassurance, guidance, and friendship to other parents as they navigate their own unique journeys.

Stories can also help us to understand ourselves better. As you read each story, some points may resonate a lot, others much less so. You may wholeheartedly agree with some ideas and fundamentally disagree with others, and that is fine. We do not expect you to engage with and act on everything you read. Rather, we encourage you to explore each story with a curious mindset, moving away from any fear of being right and wrong and instead reflecting on the things that genuinely matter most to you.

Some of the subjects we discuss may be triggering. Please be aware that this book should not replace the need to seek medical or therapeutic advice as required. We have included a comprehensive list of further resources at the end of the book which we encourage you to access for additional support.

You may not connect with everything we have shared. Our hope in creating a book full of personal stories is that its honesty and diversity affirms that there is no one way of parenting, but many. And so, we will leave you with this: what is the one thing you will take from this book that will support you to feel more empowered in your parenting choices?

Chapter 1

PARENTING OURSELVES BEFORE WE PARENT OUR CHILDREN

Chandrika Iyer

"Like every parent, I want nothing so much as my children's well-being. I want it so badly I may actually succeed in turning myself into a contented and well-adjusted person, if only for my children's sake."

—Joyce Maynard

In my 35 years of experience as an educator and later as a parent coach, supporting parents, children, and young adults across many cultures and countries, the one common feature I have recognized is how many parents seek to parent by doing the opposite! For example, if their parents were demanding of them, they strive to be more lenient with their children. If they were overindulged as children, they are now stricter as parents. If they faced academic pressure, they wish to just let their children be.

This plays out in different ways. Some people continue with the same choices made by their parents, some take "doing the opposite" to extremes, some consciously try and hold onto what serves them well, and many realize that even though they try very deliberately to "not be like their parents," there are times when they behave exactly in the way they had vowed never to act!

This is one of the main reasons we all need to grow up again by parenting ourselves before we turn to the responsibility of raising our children. To heal from all our fears, anxieties, hurts, anger, disappointments, sadness, and trauma, lest we inadvertently pass it all onto the next generation.

Growing up, I internalized beliefs, some of which I held onto and others I let go of. Here are a few of them.

1. To feel valued, loved, and "good enough," I had to consistently succeed in whatever I did. No matter what, I had to win to gain that recognition from my parents and teachers.

2. Making mistakes was awful; it meant I had somehow "failed."

3. I could make my teachers and parents "like" me if I obeyed them and pleased them by doing what they asked, even if I did not want to do it. I still carry this guilt with me from nearly 45 years ago, when my teacher asked me to get a cane to beat my classmate who had done poorly on the test. I hated doing it but did it anyway, and even though I know it was not my fault, I still feel pained to think about it.

4. I am capable and can achieve my goals if I work hard.

Although I was a high achiever, some of these beliefs made me anxious. As a young mother, I do know that I passed on some of these anxieties to my children without even being aware of them. I will share more on this later. Nevertheless, looking back, I am grateful that they taught me the values of honesty, responsibility, commitment, and hard work. These are all learnings that I have taken through making space to reflect openly and non-judgmentally on my own parenting journey over the years.

***

Parenting does not come with a manual and a "one book fits all" approach. Though I read Dr. Benjamin M. Spock's bestseller *The Common Sense Book of Baby and Child Care*, the go-to book for new parents in the 1980s, nothing of what I read prepared me for the actual work of parenting. When my daughter was born at 23, I felt overwhelmed, tired, confused, and in pain and discomfort. I did not find breastfeeding a life-changing experience as many mothers I knew had described it. For me, it was painful and tedious. I loved my baby, but it was not what I had imagined, just cooing and cuddling, easy to handle, all very hunky-dory. It took me a few weeks and perhaps a few years to fully comprehend the enormity of this responsibility!

I vividly recall the first thought that crossed my mind when my daughter was born. It was a prolonged labour, and I asked my doctor, "Is my baby ok?" And there it was, the worrying! Every parent on this planet has, at one point or the other, felt worried about their child. At that moment, I could truly resonate with what my mother would feel when she sometimes said she was worrying about my siblings or me—trivial matters, in my opinion. I would tell her off and ask her to stop overthinking! And yet, here I was, a brand-new mother, and the first thing I did was to express concern for my newborn: *Is she ok?* And at that precise moment, it hit home, I had now become a parent!

***

I do have a lot of happy memories of my childhood. I often reflect on my family of origin because it is important to recognize, claim, and celebrate all the joys and, at the same time, those aspects which did not work well. There is no doubt that we carry both the joys and the hurts into our adulthood. And sometimes we do the very same things we had vowed never to do if we became parents!

I am the oldest of three siblings, and we were all born within 5 years of our parent's marriage. I can only imagine the stress and strain on my mother, who was just 26 years old with three young children to look after. My father would be at work most of the day, so the task of child-rearing was mostly my mother's. Right from an early age, I remember having to be the "responsible" one. I remember my grandmother once saying to my grandfather that even as a 5-year-old, I had always been treated as a grown-up, even though I was still a child.

I had to outperform my siblings to get any attention from my mother. Growing up, this meant that I had to perform well and "come first" in everything I did, whether they be school grades, music competitions, essay writing, debates, or drama, and I was constantly compared with peers and pushed to prove that I could do better than them. All I knew then was the only way I could get much-needed recognition from my mother was by pleasing her and doing well to avoid her anger and my fears. My mother was ambitious for me and believed in me. Today, if I am confident, the credit goes primarily to her. But unfortunately, the pressure to perform well also made me feel anxious a lot of the time, and this anxiety continued into adulthood.

Growing up, we were also not allowed to make any decisions or have choices. We were just told what to do and had to "obey." We were never allowed to question these decisions as it was considered disrespectful. I was compelled to learn Carnatic music and a musical instrument but never encouraged to play a sport. In many cultures, it is thought that when children voice their opinions or choices, they are being rude. Obedience is sometimes equated to respect.

Reading Carol Dweck's book *Mindset* made me realize that in my family we had often lived by our "fixed mindset." My father would remark that I needed to improve at math or state that I would not do well in the subject as I was so slow. It made me think of myself as never able to do well in math. Even though I could do math, I never considered putting in the effort as, in my head, it had to come easy, or if it did not, it meant I was no good at it. It was the same mindset in school. Our report cards either said we were "good" or "poor" in subjects. Labels stick! And they are very difficult to erase, even as adults. I am sure my father did not mean for me to give up, but he told me what his teachers had said, *you are good at math only if you solve problems correctly and quickly!* The quicker you solve, the more "intelligent" you are.

***

Even though I did not consciously compare my children with those of others, I would do so indirectly. For example, I would say, "So and so's child has come first in their class," or "I heard that your friend secured full marks in her math test." I know I was trying to motivate them and do my best, as many parents do, but it certainly was not the "best" way. Most parents, including my parents, are well-meaning and want to do their best for their children. But frequently, we need more skills to offer our children the right kind of nurture and structure. Our parenting is often uneven because what may have served us well may not do for our children, and thus we need to learn what to hold onto and what to let go of. No doubt, this requires self-awareness, effort, support, and compassion.

The one thing I did, which I had vowed never to do with my children, was to shame them when they did not do well or made choices that did not work out. When shamed, children grow up with the belief that they are not good enough; it makes them timid and seeps into their persona in many insidious ways. When I recognized this behavior was not serving me or my children well, I began consciously allowing my children to make their choices and take responsibility for them—without fear of shame or attribution. This was an important personal lesson: the value gained from being open to constantly adapting my parenting style. I did not need to get it right first time; how I responded to and grew from my reflections along the way is what mattered. My daughter is now following this with her children, which is probably a parenting experience she has decided to keep from her upbringing!

From the start of my parenting journey, I decided to do my best to love my children unconditionally. I found this very challenging because the love I had received growing up was more conditional. Being able to separate the child from the behavior can be difficult. We tend to label the child rather than the behavior. Parents often label their children lazy, selfish, or ungrateful when it is the child's behavior that has presented in this way. Still, the child gets labelled in the process! Recognizing and challenging this was especially important to how I wanted to be as a parent, and so I would constantly remind myself of my mantra—*I wish to love my children unconditionally*—so that it was always front of mind.

My daughter now has her children, and I see her parenting my granddaughters with much more patience than I ever had with her at that age. I was with her when my second granddaughter was born and complimented her on her patience with the newborn. She thanked me and said, *yes, that's also because you were so impatient with us growing up. I had decided long ago that when I had children, I would try to be calm and patient with them!* Each new generation of parents has an opportunity to grow from their experiences of being raised by the last.

***

In my work now as a parent coach, I encourage parents to reflect on their "beliefs" and "values" and what they would like to inculcate in their children. Also, to consider the notion that some beliefs that served them well as children may not help them or their family today. In a recent conversation with a mother, she told me how growing up, she was not interested in studies and was more of an outdoors person. Her parents had allowed her to be the way she wanted, giving her the confidence to become who she is today. Now as a mother, she did the same for her children but feels that, perhaps, she should have encouraged her children to also focus on academics as she can see that it is quite a struggle for them to study for their exams or understand the rationale for studying subjects they do not "like." Parenting choices that served us well when we were young will not always be the right choices for our children. It can be valuable to give time to reflect on this and the extent to which we may be parenting on autopilot based on our experiences of the past.

My friend, who made the best effort to be a conscious parent, told me of an incident with her daughter. When they moved to a new country, she often worried if her teenage daughter could find her way to university using public transport. She became even more worried after reading some reports of offensive behavior on some bus routes. Each time her daughter left home, she would ask her to be careful and call her once she reached her destination. After a couple of weeks, her daughter asked her to stop doing this. She explained how she felt anxious whenever she traveled because she was always being asked to be careful. My friend's intention was certainly not to make her daughter feel anxious! She had thought she was conveying a message to make her feel safe, but instead, she had passed on her anxiety. After a few months, her daughter received a letter from the police complimenting her for reporting a person who had engaged in lewd remarks and created a nuisance on the bus.

I remember my 12-year-old client's mother who was anxious about sending her son for the first time to a summer camp. Her son was diagnosed with mild ADHD and had difficulty following instructions or tidying. Imagine her surprise when she received a letter from the organizers praising her son for all the hard work he had put in and even lauding him for keeping a tidy space!

Being a parent is one long guessing game! We need to learn how what we say is perceived by our children, and recognize that while we might say one thing, our children may assume it is something else! We need to continue to be mindful of how our beliefs could be influencing their actions and watch out for any unhelpful assumptions on both sides. We need to check-in on whether our behaviors are supporting or hindering our children to live by the values we wish to inspire. It is not easy; listening, patience and an openness to learn from our children is key.

One of the essential beliefs to encourage in children is to help them and show them how capable they are. To consciously instil the belief—I AM CAPABLE. That they are capable of coping with whatever comes their way, capable of hard work, capable of learning from their mistakes, capable of taking care of themselves, capable of tolerating frustration, capable of moving through failure, capable of facing fear, and still, as we advance, capable of meeting life with all the curveballs, the winding and straight paths.

***

As parents, to begin to unpack our beliefs, we must ask ourselves what makes us angry, frustrated, anxious, guilty, ashamed, or unhappy about our children. What beliefs do we still need to examine and modify? Can we extend ourselves the self-compassion needed to explore how these beliefs may be helping or hindering the parent we want to be and the relationship we wish to have with our kids?

Let us look at some parental emotions that hold the potential to come in the way of our self-regulation.

- GUILT: We attribute all outcomes to our behavior as parents. If our child fails a test, we are at fault. If our child has been influenced by their peers to either smoke, drink, or use substances, we blame ourselves for these issues.

- ANGER: Children must do as we say. When parenting is a top-down process, it becomes authoritarian and power-centric. Growing up, these children may become submissive, rebellious, or diffident adults.

- FEAR and ANXIETY: We fear for our children and catastrophize about the "what ifs!" This can be triggered by external factors such as news stories on violence and school shootings or bullying.

- LOW FRUSTRATION TOLERANCE: We feel that parenting should not be this hard and want or demand that it be easy.

If we experience one or more of the above emotions strongly and/or regularly, it may feel like a struggle to self-regulate. Examining some beliefs that could underlie these emotions is essential. I will briefly look at some of these beliefs.

A few beliefs underlying GUILT:

- If I make a mistake, it will always affect my child.

- I am the sole cause of my child's problems.

- My child is suffering because of my inadequacies.

A few beliefs underlying ANGER:

- My child must always listen to me and do as I say.

- Children who misbehave must be punished to avoid future failures.

- I know what is best for my child.

A few beliefs underlying FEAR and ANXIETY:

- The world is dangerous, and I must always be aware of this.

- What if something terrible happens to my child?

- I cannot help worrying about my child; worrying is a sign of good parenting.

A few beliefs underlying LOW FRUSTRATION TOLERANCE:

- I cannot stand my child's attitude and behavior.

- Other people's children do not misbehave like mine.

- What am I missing? There must be a solution that I just cannot see.

No one parent parents the same. Every parent has been parented differently and comes with their own underlying beliefs. Bringing the focus back to the values we wish to live by and instil helps to positively challenge the beliefs that could otherwise hold us back. It is this awareness that allows us to make the choices that best serve us and our children today.

When there are two parents in the family unit, or multiple caregivers present in a child's life, there can be differences in parenting methods. As parents, we must decide on the values we want to role model to our children and use these to offer them consistency. Responsibility, honesty, kindness, love, commitment, friendliness, respect, courage, compassion, mindfulness, generosity—how can we inculcate the values that are most important to us in our parenting? What beliefs and emotions are coming in the way of our self-regulation? How can we make some of these beliefs less rigid? How can we let go of some no longer valid in our lives?

In my parent sessions, I often ask—*When your children leave home, what do you expect from them?* I get many answers—"We want them to do well, have successful careers, good health, and have a loving family life." *And what else would you expect from them? Would you like them to remember your birthday? Call to wish you well? Would you want them to visit you as often as they can? Or call to check in? Make time to take you to the doctor for a check-up? Ask your grandchildren to talk to you every Sunday for a few minutes?* If your answers to all the above are yes, the work starts from the day they are born!

***

In my work, I have seen conflicts arise between parents and children because they feel that their parents do not follow all the values that they espouse but expect their progeny to do so. For example, a teenage client constantly argues with his parents about his time on his mobile. He reasons that even though his parents say he must be responsible about the time spent on his phone, he does not see the same value in his parents. If he is not allowed to use his phone after 10 p.m., he wants his parents to follow the same rule. I have teenage clients who often feel that their parents do not speak the truth. The other day my client said to me—"My dad is such a liar; while in the car, he got a phone call and said he was in a meeting. And expects me to speak the truth when he does not!"

Parenting is challenging because we are constantly being watched by our children. Children are always aware of their parent's behavior, and although few may voice it, they know when something is not right. To me, this highlights the great importance in having open and honest conversations with children from an early age about the values you wish to live by as a family. This creates accountability on both sides and encourages more positive and productive conversations between family members when someone feels another's actions violate a shared value. Rather than keeping unhelpful beliefs and assumptions bottled up inside, it is often much healthier to get them out in the open.

As parents, we all make mistakes, and it happens because we are all imperfectly human! Many parents are riddled with guilt for their parenting choices and beat themselves up for it. Looking back, one always wishes to turn back the clock and do it differently. The critical thing to remember is that, at the time, you did the best you could, and that is all you could do. You did not know better. It is never too late to make amends, say sorry, and discuss such issues with your children. Parenting guilt-free makes the process much more enjoyable.

Most parents tell me that they want their children to be good human beings. And to do that, each parent must define what this means for them.

- What is the best nurture and structure you can offer?

- What barriers, beliefs, thoughts, feelings, hurts, and trauma must you work on and heal?

- Can you let go of something that did not serve you well?

- Can you practice being more mindful of your emotions?

- Can you offer unconditional love to yourself?

- Can you forgive?

- Can you integrate the parenting you received in ways that brings value to your family today, whilst letting go of past beliefs and experiences that do not?

I believe that children come into our lives as our spiritual guides. They continuously hold a mirror reflecting our inner selves, which compels us to face ourselves and look at who we are, what we are, and how we are, not just as parents but also as human beings.

To me, the parenting journey is spiritual. I now truly understand what my grandmother said; that children are God's blessings. They are, indeed! We are given this wonderful opportunity to grow into becoming who we are meant to be as parents and as humans: joyous, compassionate, grateful to know that we are allowed to make mistakes, are sometimes allowed to get angry, feel disappointed, hurt, guilty, sad, that we are doing our best and can do better! We are, after all, fallible human beings, and there is no such thing as perfect parents or parenting! Nevertheless, the journey is fulfilling because of love, heartache, hope, growth, and many imperfections.

NOTES

1. The term "beliefs" is used in the context of Cognitive Behavior Therapy (CBT). Beliefs are stable and often unconscious assumptions about ourselves, others, and the world. As a result, our beliefs influence how we think, feel, and behave.

2. The term "values" is used in the context of Acceptance and Commitment Therapy (ACT). Values are your heart's deepest desires for how you want to behave as a human being. They describe how you want to treat yourself, others, and the world around you. There is no list of "the right" values; there are no "right" or "wrong" ones. It is like your taste in ice cream. If you prefer chocolate, but someone else prefers vanilla, that does not mean their taste is correct, and yours is wrong—or vice-versa. It just means you have different tastes.

3. A "fixed mindset" (as referenced in the chapter) is when we believe our abilities are fixed, so if you are not good at something, you might believe you will never be good at it. A "growth mindset," on the other hand, is when we believe that our abilities can change and talents develop over time.

Chapter 2

RAISING HAPPY KIDS AND BALANCING A MEANINGFUL CAREER

Jayne Ruff

"Let go of who you think you're supposed to be, embrace who you are."

—Brené Brown

"I don't want to do this anymore"—I never thought I would say this about a career I had given so much energy and time to over the years before the children came. Then motherhood changed me. I felt caught between two worlds, caught up in conflicting thoughts and feelings. I wanted to find my place as a parent and a professional but, in my first few months back to work after maternity leave, my route to get there remained unclear.

This was something I was prepared for, in theory. As an organizational psychologist, I was acutely aware of the personal challenges facing working parents; the opposing priorities, the impact on confidence, and the emotional struggles that accompany the transition back to work and beyond. There are, of course, many external pressures that must also be navigated: rising childcare costs, unsupportive organizational cultures, and wider societal assumptions and expectations. Despite my academic knowledge and experience working with others through change, for me, the reality of facing these challenges in practice was quite different.

***

My professional self has always been important to me. Becoming a psychologist was my first dream ahead of becoming a mother. It was (and still is) a big part of who I am. But when my son was born, my work identity was suddenly muted. My love and attention became fully focused on my child as I also slowly developed confidence as a new parent.

I then went back to work when my son was 8 months old. I constantly fretted about the practical challenges and logistics. But what hit me hardest was my battle with feelings of self-doubt, guilt, and uncertainty, all mixed into the new motherhood cocktail of extreme tiredness, conflicting advice, and fluctuating hormones (and not helped by the tears at childcare drop-off and pick-up!). Innocent comments from childcare staff about my son being the youngest baby in his room would hit me hard, and I would dwell on the decisions I had made about my career and my parenting.

I felt lucky to have enjoyed over half a year with my son compared with friends living elsewhere in the world, and I was aware of my privilege in having the financial means to step away from work for so long. Yet, I also felt guilty returning to work as a mother in the UK where statutory maternity leave is 52 weeks, and many of the new friends that I had made through baby groups still had months left at home. I felt anxious when I thought about the end of this unequivocal time with my little boy, and fearful of the impact this change might have on him, our relationship, and his longer-term happiness.

During these first few weeks, I continued to question my ability to operate at work with the clarity I once had, even though my results suggested otherwise. Outwardly I was smiling, while under the surface I still battled with the voices in my head shouting: "You do not have a choice but to go back to work," "You cannot be the parent you want to be anymore," "You are a bad mother for going back to work," "You are a bad co-worker for giving less time to the job."

I was operating in survival mode. Like a hamster spinning its wheel, I put in all the hours I could manage at work and home and still found myself questioning whether I was living up to expectations in either role. It was exhausting and overwhelming, and I found it very difficult to see past my emotions.

"I don't want to do this anymore." Was this truly how I felt about a career I previously enjoyed so much? Did it have to be one or the other?

***

If I could have turned the psychologist lens inwards, I would have told myself that with change as significant as becoming a parent, and then returning to work, it is normal to experience all these feelings of upheaval. My sense of self—and the identity I connected with pre-children—was being challenged and needed to evolve. But at the time I was too emotionally entangled in what felt like an intense tug-of-war between two important life areas to see this.

This was not helping me to be the parent or the professional I wanted to be. The constant undercurrent of worry meant that I was not fully present with my son or fully focused on my work. I regret not giving myself permission to just be in the moment when at home and work without interference from my inner thoughts, but I also understand why that was and very often still is difficult to achieve.

Something had to change, and the catalyst that made me take a much-needed step back was the global Covid-19 pandemic. This was a difficult time at work and home. I was unclear what the impact would be on my business—a boutique consultancy that I run alongside just one other person. I had no formal childcare and no clarity on when this essential support would resume. The work and home life juggle intensified in a way I had never experienced before, and this way of living was not sustainable. It forced me to slow down and consciously consider: *What really matters to me and my family?*

At a time when the world felt like it had turned upside down, I found great comfort in indulging in the little pleasures in life. Stepping away from the pressures of work to enjoy some fresh air and quality time together in our garden (which—living in London—we were incredibly fortunate to have) re-energized the whole family during this difficult period. Making dinner together as a couple once our toddler had gone to bed helped my partner and I recharge and reconnect after a busy day juggling both our jobs and childcare. Allocating time to my personal development through completing online courses during lockdowns re-ignited my passion for work.

These small but significant actions helped me, and my family, re-fill our happiness cups and find balance through unusual circumstances, and I wanted to take the positive learnings from this period of upheaval and uncertainty forward. Returning to my psychology roots, I started exploring what it means to experience "happiness" and how it applies to raising children and finding work-life balance. I realized that many of those little pleasures that brought us joy also served a deeper purpose—they were everyday ways of living by our values.

I am a strong advocate in my work as a psychologist that living according to your values is a fundamental factor in the pursuit of happiness, and I passionately believe that lasting happiness occurs when we invest our energy in meaningful goals across the different areas of our lives that are important to us. I am a big believer in the work of psychologists such as Steven Hayes, the co-developer of Acceptance and Commitment Therapy on which a lot of my personal and professional practices are based. It is a philosophy that I also want to role model to my children. But my experience of returning to work and then parenting through the pandemic also made me appreciate that times of change and uncertainty can be both the destabilizer that throws us off track, and the motivator that helps us to re-focus on the things we really care about today.

***

It is very difficult to tap into these values when our focus is on what needs to be done—the seemingly endless to-do lists, looming work deadlines, and mounting piles of washing. That sense of overwhelm is blinding. We also bring a lot of external influence into parenthood; the values of our parents that shaped our upbringing, our education, societal norms, and expectations around what it means to parent effectively—including how long you should take for parental leave, the childcare choices you should make and when you should go back to work. These outside pressures can sometimes lead us to act in ways that do not align with the person we want to be. We buy into the "need to have it all" mentality when, instead of trying to do everything, it is often more fulfilling to focus on what we genuinely care about.

To positively disrupt these thinking patterns in myself, I sat in my home office with a coffee one morning and reflected on the personal qualities I most want to bring to my work life and my home life. I wrote freely—without overthinking the exercise—to see what most naturally came to mind. I thought about what I would most want those closest to me to say about the way I show up for them as a daughter, a wife, a colleague, a friend, and—of course—a parent. I captured the five qualities I value most at home and work into two short, memorable lists—scribbled on two Post-it notes. There were some differences, but a lot of similarities as well. I call this my values compass. It is unique to me, based on the things that matter most in this chapter of my life today. The realization that I can choose my own direction of travel guided by my inner compass was incredibly liberating. It helped me to break away from the "comparison trap" so many parents fall into and instead stay tuned into the steps that I wanted to take.

My values compass helped me navigate my return to work after the birth of my second child with greater self-compassion and kindness, and it continues to provide a guiding light through the ups and downs of working parenthood. Running a small business on top of all the other demands of work and family life is not without its challenges, but there is an energy and excitement that I get from working toward something that I care about—one of my primary drivers is working with others to create a positive impact. This helps me stay tuned into what signifies a fulfilling work-life balance for me. Having clarity on our family values also helps me to make more conscious choices about how I balance parenting with my career.

Truthfully, there are still plenty of times when my mind tunes back into that well-known inner voice telling me: *I just can't do anything right at home or at work.* This sense that I am losing control often comes when I am juggling too much—agreeing to far too many work and home life commitments, working multiple projects while the children have chicken pox, even writing a chapter for a book on top of my day job has sparked familiar feelings of overwhelm! Sometimes, I just do not get my work and home life balance right.

What I am growing better at is recognizing the point when my balance has tipped and I am feeling stressed, then taking some small, values-led steps to help me course-correct. It is not easy, and sometimes I will spend a few days (or longer) in a bit of an emotional black hole while I try to find my route out. I am incredibly conscientious, driven, determined, and a natural doer who is not used to saying no, not today (or even next month or next year!). I do not like to let other people down. I have to fight my gravitational pull to take on more and find peace with good being good enough. When I do take this step back, I feel the benefit of re-orientating toward the things that I personally care about and putting my time and energy there. Rather than apologizing for what I am not doing, I try to recognize and celebrate everything that I am achieving. Just like building physical strength, developing these mental muscles is an ongoing commitment and I am trying to work on it in little ways daily.

Often this comes down to routine decisions and actions. It is the accumulation of small, meaningful acts that brings my family greater fulfilment over and above any single lifestyle choice, and I have become better at recognizing and celebrating these. I am my best at home when I am a good listener to my children and my partner. To live by this value, I resist the temptation to check work e-mails on my phone in the short hours between childcare pick-up and bedtime. This time is precious. I will play with my kids, and watch TV, snuggled closely together because that is often what they most want to do after a long day. I will ask my pre-schooler to share stories about his day, which is a subtle way of encouraging him to think about his values too, and I will tell him tales from mine. Often these chats last no longer than a few minutes. I have come to appreciate that it is the quality of connection in these moments that is most crucial to supporting my children's happiness over the quantity of time I can give to them at the end of the working day.

My partner and I try to take a 10-minute walk together with a coffee on days when we are both working from home. A warm hug before we leave in the morning and when we get back from the office reminds us that we are in it together as a team, and every few months, we treat ourselves to a day off during the working week to spend extra quality time together when the kids are in childcare. These moments are small, but the positive impact is significant.

I am my best at work when I set personal goals that align with my values. It is a different way of thinking about prioritization. These values-based actions can be small or big. A small action I am working toward is to protect a little time in my work diary to network because I value connecting with and learning from others. During the Covid-19 pandemic, I set up another arm of my business specifically focused on supporting working parents at an individual, managerial, and organizational level—aligning my passions in psychology and parenting with my desire to drive positive change in workplaces. While it has not been easy, the sense of purpose it gives me is powerful. There are still elements of my work that do not bring me joy; that I just need to do. There are also parts of parenting I find more pleasurable than others; I do not think anyone relishes toddler tantrums! But it is the goals aligned with my values that keep me motivated, even on the days when I am sleep deprived.

I am mindful that my children are still very young; the attention they require from me at this age is different from the support they will need in 10 years. I have plenty of time to continue developing my career as my children grow, and I have become better at managing my expectations about what is currently feasible. At the same time, I do still question whether I have what it takes to run a business and be there for my family. It is yet another familiar story that my mind likes to revisit: *Do you have the tenacity to be a businesswoman and a mum? What do others have that you don't...? What do other children get from their mothers that they won't get from you?*

Often it shows up when my work-life balance is once again being challenged in some way, which is a fairly regular occurrence when running two businesses while parenting a 1- and 4-year-old! An important step in managing this has been to accept that what I protect and prioritize may look quite different from the choices of others. I will often ask myself: "Where can I add the greatest value in the time, and with the energy, I have to give today?" This simple question helps me to take small, meaningful steps forward while acknowledging that I do not need to have it all right now.

***

I am very aware that an area of my life where I would like to give greater focus is my health and well-being—like many parents I tend to put myself at the bottom of the priority list! I have a lot of work still to do here, but I am trying to take even the smallest of steps forward by making some conscious choices aligned with my health values. At the same time, I actively try to step away from any internal or external pressures that I may feel to be a particular way (like returning to my pre-baby body)—something that often takes conscious effort when surrounded by perfect Instagram accounts. I also have a handful of simple rituals that help me switch from home to work mode and back again. Listening to an industry podcast after the childcare drop-off eases me back into my work mindset. My partner and I protect certain evenings to relax together while allowing some flexibility to extend the workday if needed when we recognize it will ease the pressure elsewhere. I am limiting work travel while my children are young to be more available but this boundary, and others, may evolve.

Beyond boundaries, there are times when I need to make tough decisions about what to prioritize across work and home life. I might turn down a lucrative work project if it would infringe too heavily on my family values. I might work late into the evenings on a project I am passionate about, which will come at a cost to my personal life. These choices are never easy and often trigger a lot of different emotions: guilt, fear, exhaustion, and doubt. But I do have a choice, and that is one of the most important lessons I have learned about being a working parent. This has helped me to ruminate less over whether the decisions I make are "right" or "wrong" because ultimately, I still control what I let in and keep out.

I try not to make these decisions alone. My partner and I regularly talk through scenarios where our work life and home life values feel at odds. These are often just quick, 2-minute conversations once the kids are in bed, and we almost never find the perfect answer. But the power comes from having the conversation, even if sometimes these are just about having a moan, letting off steam, and getting the whirring thoughts out of our heads and into a safe space. It helps us acknowledge the pressure points, get a different perspective on possible solutions and stay attuned to the current needs of our family and each other. I seek advice from close friends too. When appropriate, I will also share the reasons for my choices with my children, because I believe open and honest communication is important in building our family trust and overall happiness.

My working parenthood journey continues to be a winding emotional path of change. Each new turn has the potential to influence my direction of travel. The bumps in the road often lead me to question whether I have my work-life balance right. I am tired. I am not always as patient as I would like to be. I miss having the time to exercise, relax and meet up with friends. I miss my children when I am at work. Traversing the pressures of hectic work and home life is tough. Those simple pleasures that became habits during pandemic lockdowns require a lot more conscious thought now that the world's "normal" has resumed and many more distractions are vying for our attention and time. But it is the appreciation of the power of conscious awareness that I try to hold onto today. You cannot change what you cannot see, and I am grateful to have discovered ways of noticing the internal and external blockers I was largely unaware of—or too busy to spot—before.

***

I have come to realize that the best way to find a meaningful path around potential roadblocks is to decelerate, and I have achieved this through everyday mindfulness—which I like to think of as simply stopping more frequently to take a breath. I was fortunate enough to have an uncomplicated birth experience with both my children, and within this context, I was able to explore the use of breathwork and present-moment awareness. Subsequently, the value of conscious awareness has become a much greater focus in my everyday work and home life. Mindfulness involves focusing on the present moment and observing thoughts, feelings, and emotions without judgment or analysis. While it sounds counterintuitive, the ability to accept every thought, feeling, and emotion—even the unpleasant ones—is part of our route to happiness. This acceptance helps to release the hold negative emotions might have.

The value of mindfulness can be experienced in just a few minutes. Simply drawing attention to my breath, the sensations in my body, and my surroundings can help me quickly re-calibrate my emotions, whether I am facing overload at work or frustration when my boys just will not go to sleep. Rather than being stuck on the hamster wheel, I have become better at noticing the physical cues that indicate my balance might be about to tip, like a tightening sensation in my chest. I am also more conscious of the actions I might take to unhelpfully divert attention away from these feelings, such as reaching for the sweet treats in my cupboard that offer a temporary sugar high.

Acknowledging and labeling my emotions, rather than suppressing or struggling against them, lets me choose how I interact with them. I often ask myself questions such as: *Is this thought or feeling helping me to be the person I ideally want to be? What is this thought or feeling trying to tell me is most important?* Taking this moment's pause slows down my mind, and racing heartbeat, and lets me untangle from unhelpful internal noise. I have come to accept that there will be times when I feel overwhelmed by work and family life. This is not a case of submission. Rather, acknowledging the challenges has allowed me to make more conscious choices about how I engage with these feelings when they arise.

I might feel guilty about leaving work early to collect my sons from childcare but being present at the end of their day is important to me. I would rather pick up work again in the evening once they have gone to bed if needed. I might feel guilty about a night away from my family for work but as I value being ambitious, on occasions this may be the right choice to make. With my values compass in hand, I am better equipped to stay on track.

Being more connected to the present moment has aided my parenting too. My toddler gives his undivided attention to a bird eating crumbs on a picnic bench, and I like to join in. My preschooler and I lie in bed together for just a few minutes before the day begins. We will talk about what we can see and hear—traffic outside the window, his little brother babbling downstairs, creaking and cracking I might not otherwise notice. These simple activities invigorate me, and I can see that it is these precious little moments that bring my children happiness too. I hope that making time for and involving my children in these small mindfulness practices will encourage a healthy relationship with their own emotions and benefit their longer-term well-being.

What is more, slowing down to acknowledge all the feelings in our household has also raised my awareness of the often-subtle feedback clues my boys give me about how they are experiencing our family's work-life dynamic. I listen to the words they use and the questions they ask. I watch what they do and the scenarios they choose to role-play. I aim to offer them a constant safe space where they can speak freely about their emotions—the good and the bad. If I could recommend one small change every parent could make to their daily routine to raise happy kids, it would be to spend just a few minutes longer listening, observing, and talking to each other.

***

They say the key to lifelong happiness is making small tweaks on a regular basis. I have grown in my job since becoming a parent by prioritizing what really matters, and I believe I am a better parent for having work as another dimension in my life. I try to recognize and celebrate the strengths I bring to both roles, many of which have been enhanced through parenthood. I am now much more content with the perception of myself as a constant work-in-progress. I am also mindful that my children will continue to grow in body and mind, and so what brings them happiness will evolve.

I am excited to continue this journey of discovery with my children. I have become much more aware of the influence my values will have on their beliefs, and that I can play a proactive role in helping them to explore and shape their values as they grow. I am still figuring out what this path looks like for us as a family; perhaps more frequent conversations about the values we share and those that are different, what it means to act by our values and how to support each other in this, and how to recognize and respond when a value is compromised. I would like to define shared values and find simple ways to connect with these on a regular basis to help us navigate through family life, together.

I believe that the secret to having a successful career and raising happy kids simultaneously is to focus on purpose. I hope that taking a values-led approach to my work-life balance demonstrates to my sons a different measure of success that celebrates acting by what is personally important, above external validation. I will also continue to encourage them to embrace their emotions in the pursuit of the values that define their meaningful life and help them to see all the little ways they demonstrate their personal strengths and unique qualities each day.

Authenticity is a cornerstone of mental health, well-being, and contentment. Work-life balance is a very personal thing; there's no one-size-fits-all solution. The best piece of advice I can offer for making conscious choices that will lead to happier kids while balancing a career is to cut out the noise and stay tuned into what really matters to you and your family.

Chapter 3

PARENTING AND LEARNING FROM OUR HERO, A SPECIAL NEEDS CHILD

Yagya Mahadevan

"Until you have a kid with special needs you have no idea of the depth of your strength, tenacity and resourcefulness."

—Anonymous

I did not fully appreciate the meaning and magnitude of the word "responsibility" until October 3, 2010, 8:30 a.m. Adhruth was born at 7:42 a.m. and then immediately admitted into the neonatal intensive care unit. At 8:30 a.m. I filled in his admission form. Answering my relationship to the patient, when, for the first time in my life I wrote "Father," I became acutely aware of a new responsibility. And what a proud moment it was... I did not realize how much our lives would change forever.

Today, Adhruth is an energetic, bubbly, ever-smiling, happy 12-year-old child diagnosed with autism. He is non-verbal and formula-fed through a gastronomy tube (G-tube) in his stomach which gives him 60 percent of his daily nutritional needs. He has been diagnosed with hearing loss and has undergone surgery on his head to correct Chiari Malformation Decompression. He needs medication at night for sleep. But none of this stops him from living a happy life and being a great teacher for us.

***

For Adhruth, his mother comes first, father later.

As is the custom in India, we did not know if our baby was a boy or girl and so we did not finalize any name. When he was born, Adhruth did not have a name to refer to him. In the hospital, he was always "Baby of Subhashree," in every interaction, be it medical exams, or tests. Even though he has my name in his last name now and will have it for his life, during that initial period of his life, the medical profession referred to him only through his mother who carried him in her tummy for 10 months and brought him into the world. It was not "Baby of Yagya" or "Baby Mahadevan" (with my last name), it was always "Baby of Subhashree." Society cares more about the father by adding that name, the medical profession appreciates the contribution of the mother right away. Adhruth's birth made me recognize and appreciate this too.

Not all of us humans travel at the same speed.

This is a thought that has often been explained by my Guru, Mahatria. Just because you are driving slowly, it does not mean you will not reach your destination. You may reach the destination a little bit later than someone going faster than you, but you will reach the destination if you keep your focus on the road.

My son Adhruth too taught me this in his first few years. As is normal, within the family there was a lot of discussion about milestones. "Has your son started doing this?" "At this age, they are supposed to do that." No, Adhruth did not meet any milestones of typical children. It took him a long time to sit on his hip and not fall. It was not that he never sat down, he took his time. We were impatient and concerned. We did not know what was happening. Social pressure started taking a toll on us, but this is when we realized he was on his own path, journey, and speed. He was not running to be first anywhere. He was going to keep his own pace and we as parents had to support him at every step. The comparison was making us feel bad and believe we were terrible parents. But when we changed our perspective, every milestone was a celebration and we were not bothered by how late we achieved it.

Smile, it can cure anything.

Adhruth is not bothered by his environment, what others do, what others say. He lives his life happily, in his own way. When he laughs, he really laughs! He laughs his heart out, mouth open, lips to the widest point, and his laugh is incredibly contagious.

There are days when we as his parents think of Adhruth's future, and we are worried, irritated, or get stuck in a negative thought cycle. He understands our emotions and will come close to our faces and keep his lips on our cheeks, acting as if he is kissing us, telling us—*Why are you worried?* And we laugh. If there is one medicine that can make us forget all our worries, tiredness, and negative emotions, it is his laugh.

Mahatria often says that "children do not need a reason to be happy; they can laugh for no reason." Here is Adhruth as my teacher, showing me experientially how to live a life that way, uncoupled from the belief that happiness is found in materialistic things.

It is, as if he indicates: *What about life can you change when the thing that you are trying to change is not in your control?* It is as if he wants to tell us: *Enjoy life Dad, smile at life Mom, we will do this together.*

I will live my life like Adhruth, happy and fancy-free. What a great life lesson for a father from his son, who has not spoken a word yet.

***

Decisions in life revolve around our son's health priorities.

Every decision we take in life is based on the question, *what is right for Adhruth?* We first came to the US from India for an 18-month assignment, then extended for another year, but when it was time to go back, we decided to remain in this country, the primary reason being the additional health care we were able to get for him here.

Many among our friends and family thought we wanted to stay here to make more money and maintain a good lifestyle but never understood that our priority in life was Adhruth. We decided to stay away from the city that brought us up, our roots, for the good of Adhruth. It is probable that they could not understand or relate to what we go through.

If they had not been in his shoes, they would not know. Our world being our son, we learned to ignore those who could not appreciate the decisions we took as parents.

But there was the question, was our decision-making going against nature?

During his early years, Adhruth struggled to eat food orally. He had challenges in swallowing food of many common textures. He used to drink porridge, which he likes, and that was his staple food for a few years. Due to his low muscle tone, which we identified later, he had difficulty chewing and swallowing. Thus, he did not receive most of the nutrient values of the food. Feeding him orally would be an hourly ordeal for each meal and since the quantity is low, we had to feed him four to five times in a day.

As parents, we would get upset because he was not eating enough. Adhruth would get upset because we are making him sit for long durations doing something he did not enjoy. It was painful to watch this as parents. Some people do not have enough food to feed their children. For me, the worst feeling was being in a state of helplessness where we had everything our child needed but we could not make him eat it.

It was then that doctors spoke to us about the G-tube that could be surgically added in his belly and allow us to feed in food from outside. As a child, when I did not eat fast, my grandmother would always say, I wish God would create a zipper to stuff the food inside. Here was a modified version of that for us in real time.

It was not easy for us as parents the day we heard about that. Even though the doctor said it is possible for Adhruth to outgrow the G-tube, looking at his conditions, this could be a long-term solution. We had sleepless nights over the question, *were we doing something to him that was against nature?* We were about to make medical decisions that he would carry for the long term.

The doctors helped us make a decision. They explained that currently there was pressure as parents because Adhruth was not eating enough, but then it was tremendous pressure for Adhruth because he did not enjoy the hourly ordeal. This was starting to impact the parent–child relationship, making it painful for both. Getting some medical help would maintain our relationship, and that was critical, especially since he did not have a voice to say.

Again, Adhruth tolerated the pain of surgery, showing us that he is a resolute soul and will go through everything to make things work. He started feeling something weird in his tummy and would keep checking that. He soon outgrew that and today this intervention has been one of the biggest blessings in our life. We are able to take care of his nutritional needs and build a better relationship.

***

There came the day that our voiceless boy found a voice and started becoming expressive.

There were numerous occasions when as parents we wondered if Adhruth started talking, how his voice would be. We were yearning for that sweet boy to call us Dad, Mom. We missed that part. Yes, we understood he is special, but still as parents it was not easy to come to terms with that.

Again, his teachers and therapists came to our rescue. They started motivating him to use a communication device. An iPad with an app, Proloquo2Go became his voice, his way of telling us what he wants. For example, there is an image of a blueberry and he can press that when he wants to ask for blueberries. When he wants to go and play in the swing, he has a button for that in the app as well. The teachers never gave up on the fact that he was teachable and that he would do it. Persistence helped and soon the teachers were explaining to us how he went for his iPad and pressed the button for his favorite wagon ride during free play. This is how he started to talk without his voice.

Once he learned that he could ask for his needs differently, he started being more expressive. If he wanted something, he would grab our hands, walk us to the place where his favorite things are kept, and point to us and smile. Technology became his way of talking to us. Recently I woke up to a dream of Adhruth talking and could not stop myself from thinking it will happen one day as he has surprised us repeatedly with everything.

And then there came the day when Adhruth gained a second voice.

After Adhruth was born, and once we understood his needs, we were skeptical about a second child. We knew that Adhruth would need more time and energy from us and that we would not be able to spare enough time for a second child. But we had a surprise—Avyukth, who is now 5 years old. And, he has taught us a lot about his brother. Seeing a typical child grow, we have often wondered how easy this journey has been. But at the same time, this has shown us the struggle Adhruth had to go through and the fighter that he is.

Recently, we had haircut and wash appointments for both boys back-to-back. We typically do not do this but somehow this is how the schedule worked out. Adhruth got his haircut first, and every time after a haircut his cuteness increases. The relief of taking off the additional hair shows up on his face, even though he does not complain when it grows faster.

Then came our talker's turn. He sat in the chair and started talking to the hairdresser (HD). After 10 minutes of talking back and forth, this is where it landed.

HD: How old are you?

Avy: I am 5 years old.

HD: How old is your brother?

Avy: Adhruth Anna (brother) is 12 years old.

HD: Oh. Ok. That is good.

Avy: My brother is 12 years old, but he cannot talk. He has autism and so he is still like a baby. I love him so much and he loves me.

HD: That is wonderful to hear.

Avy: Yes. I know he loves me because he lets me hug him whenever I want. He also hugs me when I go near him to tell me he loves me because he cannot talk to me about it. I love jumping and dancing in front of him to make him smile because I love to see Adhruth Anna smile and be happy always.

Standing there, I was speechless, and tears were ready to pop out of my eyes. Adhruth, through his ways had been able to make Avyukth realize that not all children have to talk.

In summer evenings, when we go for a walk around the block, Avyukth will hold Adhruth's hand and Adhruth will reach out to hold Avyukth's hand when extended and they love each other's company. Can I stretch my hand out to fellow parents who have a similar journey and vice versa? Adhruth and Avyukth show me how to be a support for each other.

***

Adhruth's teachers have never given up on him.

Adhruth has an Individualized Education Plan (IEP) in his school customized for his needs in the classroom. There is a regular review of his IEP goals, with his teacher sharing on his progress. At the very first IEP meeting, we were nervous. We did not know what to expect—we knew meeting objectives was tough for him. But they celebrated every single step he took toward progress. There were videos recorded of him doing things that he had found difficult a few months back. From walking stairs without an adult's help to picking things and dropping in a basket, requesting things through his iPad, sitting in a place for 5 minutes, indicating that he has to go to potty—everything was adored, every milestone was celebrated.

Every teacher who has crossed paths with Adhruth, spoke of how happy and smiling he is and how his smile had made their days. Teachers have walked into his classroom to get a wave, to see that smile, to feel that hug from him to make their day better. As parents, it is painful to think about a 12-year-old that needs a diaper to be changed 5 times in a day, but his teachers gave us a different way for us to see him. His teachers were not ready to give up on him even though as parents we thought he would not be able to do something. Our expectations were day to day and in the grind of the day to day, we had missed some of those happy moments, his victory laps.

We too started enjoying his milestones and took victory laps for him. Adhruth taught us to take that victory lap for every achievement. There is nothing called a small or big win. A win is a win, learn to celebrate it.

Love is not blind; it is mute in our case.

There is a lot that Adhruth does not understand when we talk, express, or do things for him. His life goes by schedules. When it is time to feed and we feed, he cannot tell us he is not hungry at this time. His life runs like clockwork. How do we explain to him we understand and love him even though he cannot understand what that means. We started saying "I love you" and hugging and cuddling him more. Now, we just have to say, "I love you Adhruth," and immediately there is a *big* smile on his face. He hugs us, keeps his lips on our cheeks, leads our hands to his head to make us pamper him, and gives us a huge laugh. Even though we have longed for years to hear him call out to us and tell us he loves us, who wants those words, when he has found his own way of expression.

He may not understand many things in his life, but he does understand *love*. That is more critical than anything else anyone can teach him. He has shown us that *love* comes before everything.

***

Where do we look for support?

We cannot always take part in friends' birthday parties, excursions, trips, and tours as we need to plan for Adhruth's feeding, medication, and needs. We prefer to plan things just for our family and must stay away from group settings.

During our weekend trips, we are used to feeding Adhruth through the G-tube in public places. Initially, we were very reluctant. What would passers-by think of us? Would they think we were not encouraging Adhruth to eat orally? Would they make fun of us? Would they tease Adhruth, because he is different? Children stare at him at times not sure what we are doing to him. One instance changed it all for us and changed my perspective completely.

At the Tulip Festival in Iowa, we were feeding Adhruth through the G-tube in a public park. A stranger was constantly looking at us. Even before he had approached us, being used to these situations, I knew he would. And then would come some advice, suggestions. I was ready with my justification of Adhruth's medical condition. But this man walked straight, sat right next to me in the grass, put his arms on my shoulder as if giving a half hug and looking right into my eyes started talking.

"As parents, both of you are doing an extraordinarily important and a great job. It is not easy to go through what you guys are going through for your son. I can understand the sacrifices you both are making to make this little boy's life better. There is only one thing I can say right now, it will all pay off for your son in years and when you look back after many years, you will feel good that you did what is right for him. Over the years, he will be better, and I can say that confidently. Look…"

He pointed his hands to a girl who was a few years older than Adhruth, and was happily playing in the garden with her family. He then continued, "That's my daughter. She was tube feeding for a long time, but that is what helped her in her growth and now she is doing great. I pray to God to give you enough strength, as that is the only thing I can do for you. Your little guy will make you proud, one day." Saying this he walked past us, not even looking at us again. We then continued to feed Adhruth, with a teary eye and a resolute heart.

Not everyone can put themselves in our shoes and understand what we go through. But this anonymous stranger was able to understand us as he has been through our journey. He is part of our family, a family of Special Parents. Through Adhruth, we know there are great, caring, wonderful people around.

Next time, when you see a child with special needs, when you walk past parents who are struggling with a child with different needs, if you have a minute, stop by. Give them a hug, a pat on their back; talk to them, show them some empathy, and tell them that they are not alone. We do not want you to be doing anything for us, but just showing us that we are not alone in this different journey means a *lot* to us.

Chapter 4

BE THE CHANGE: BRINGING UP GENDER-SENSITIVE CHILDREN

Aarthi Prabhakaran

"Girls are weighed down by restrictions, boys with demands - two equally harmful disciplines."

—Simone de Beauvoir

After multiple international relocations, we decided to relocate back to our home in India, to be closer to family and return to our roots. The year we moved back from the UK, our second-born son was in grade 2. He had benefited from the early years of UK curriculum, where concepts to understand sexuality, emotional intelligence, diversity, and inclusion, are introduced as early as kindergarten. Our move to India was a sea of change and at the beginning impacted him quite a bit.

At the community playground, he encountered a lot of gender-discriminating language such as "boys don't cry." He was called names like "cry-baby," "stupid," and "loser" because of his sensitivity. In fact, it was not long before he started internalizing the discriminating behavior himself. There was this day we had gone shopping and I picked a light pink T-shirt for him, and he said, "That's a girl's color, boys only wear blue." One would have assumed that after breaking the gender stereotypes that I had myself grown up with, and raising an older child abroad, parenting a second child would have been a breeze and gender biases would not be a thing. Yet, that seemed so far from the truth.

Parenting has always been a challenging journey for every generation of parents. In this digital age of information explosion, it has become a lot more complex. The age-old stereotypes and norms, more specifically the gender norms are deeply rooted in the patriarchal constructs, which are now being termed toxic. Our parents dealt with the constructs of male, female, and heterogeneous relationships while everything else was a taboo topic, and hence not part of mainstream discussions. Now, we have gender constructs that include terms such as binary/non-binary, transgender (or third gender), cis-gender, and probably more than what I am aware of. These are different from the assigned at birth (biological) sex. We also have sexuality, which is a person's identity in relation to the gender or genders to which they are typically attracted, vis-à-vis, their sexual orientation. This also has a multitude of taxonomy, with evolving definitions every day (see Chapter 9: Supporting Your Child If They Come Out to You). As parents, we have a responsibility to continually educate ourselves to best inform, learn from and support our children.

***

On my first international trip to the United States, as a first-time parent carrying a 5-month-old baby girl, I was forced to confront the gender stereotypes that I had internalized from my upbringing in India. As my interactions with the people in my new locale expanded, I realized what I thought of as appropriate behavior for a man and woman was deeply constricting. To take an example, I used to feel discomfort when I saw trans people and same-sex couples walking the streets; I found myself avoiding eye contact. Eventually, I realized that I did not know how to respond to them because I had never been in direct contact with people from these communities during my developmental years in India.

Being raised in India, where the gender norms are really pronounced, not just in media but also within every household, there used to be days when I felt trapped in the body that I was born in. There were restrictions imposed right from what dress I wore, how I stood or sat, whom I talked to, how I spoke and laughed, my education and career choices—a never-ending list.

As a child and adolescent, I grew up with my thoughts and beliefs strongly influenced by my Indian upbringing; despite my exposure to the diverse culture that India is known for, it is still bound largely by similar customary practices and core values. As an adult and as a first-time parent, my international travels began when my firstborn was an infant and went on for a little over a decade, within which time, I had my second child, and a few more international relocations—United States, France, and UK.

Over the years, I have been used to expressions ranging from awe to utter shock, leading to the one curious question from many inquisitive parents— "How did you manage all of this, especially with a young family?" Here is my recommendation to young parents, getting started on this journey:

To parent a child is to first (unlearn and) learn yourself, what you wish to teach the child, and then lead by example. Children always imitate what is being modelled by the adults around them.

During my second relocation within the US, with my 2-year-old toddler, I enrolled in a "Parents as Teachers" program that was run by the local community centre. We had a weekly music session and a circle time that entailed nursery rhymes, storybook reading, and some free play time. The facilitator would do home visits to educate the parents on the developmental milestones of the children and recommend books for co-reading with our child under the "Raise a Reader" program, structured for parents to model behavior and enable their children to become readers themselves.

I started reading up a lot on gender identities and the constructs, patriarchy, and its long-reaching impact on thoughts, and behaviors across generations. I started venturing outside my comfort zone and started interacting with people from different races and communities. I learned about their culture and lifestyles by spending time with them on every occasion that I could.

***

While that helped scratch the surface of these topics, I was dealing with my own blocks stemming from my conditioning and unconscious biases.

Here is an incident that helped me understand this reality. This is from a time when we lived in France, incidentally, the place where my gender awareness journey forayed into gender sensitivity and acceptance.

Both my children were in their spring break, and one fine day they decided to "pretend play." They were pretending to be me and my husband… their Mommy and Daddy! Our daughter took on Daddy's role, put on his coat, hat, and laptop bag, ready to go out to the office. Our son took up Mommy's role and requested his sister to dress him up (which she dutifully carried out) with my coat, scarf, and a grocery shopping bag.

Here is how it went:

Daddy: I am all set to leave for the office. See you in the evening.

Mommy: Take care and have a nice day.

Scene shifts to a weekend.

Mommy: I am leaving for the farmers' market.

A few seconds later, Mommy is back from shopping.

Mommy: Look how much fruit I bought.

Daddy: Oh... Let me help you carry the bag. Come in and sit down. Here, have some water and rest. Let me take care of the cooking and children.

I felt so happy, bursting with pride! How many gender stereotype barriers had we (me and my husband) broken as parents? We had been successful in breaking the stereotypical image of roles and brought in a sense of equality not just in the responsibilities of people in the house but also in what role they chose for themselves.

Just a few weeks later, there was another interesting conversation with our young children, while they were watching their favorite show, *Handy Manny*:

Me: What do you wish to be when you grow up?

Son: Tram driver.

Daughter: I don't have to be anything! Only boys need to work.

It was like someone had given us a sucker punch and left us winded and stunned.

My husband: Why do you say so?

Daughter: Amma (Mommy) is always at home and doesn't go to work. I am going to be like her.

Me: Honey, don't I work too?

Daughter: I know you do stuff inside the home, drop, and pick us up from school, care for us. That is what I will do as well when I grow up.

Me: I also do other things outside the home.

Daughter (with a look of surprise): What do you do?

I patiently explained to her the other hats I wear, including as a parenting and life skills consultant, facilitator, volunteer at community centres, an active member of the Parent Teacher Association (PTA) in their school, and an avid blogger, sharing thoughts and learnings in the hope that many generations can benefit from. She was listening intently. For someone who grew up in a culture where I was constantly told that my work should speak for itself, having to vocalize what I do was a new experience, but I had to do it to ensure that my children did not develop filtered views of the roles that I and my spouse play, based on their partial perception.

This marked the conscious exercise of sharing our daily experiences with each other as part of our family "connection ritual." As soon as the children got home from school and they were done sharing what happened during their day, I would share with them what I did for that day. This started the open communication channel within our home which set the course for many interesting conversations that followed.

Today, I am a willing learner from my children, who help me view their world where the gender constructs are unraveling, which brings with it the discussions about sexuality as well. I am happy that the roles are reversed, and my daughter now enlightens me with the expansion of LGBTQIA+ and their definitions, what cis-gendered means, and more. I am no expert on gender even now, after being a parent for 16 long years, but I do know that I have two wonderful teachers in my children.

The only way this has been possible was by working on my unconscious biases that hindered open communication on these topics in our living room. Once I addressed that, our connection rituals took care of the rest.

***

In November 2013, I received an email from my daughter's grade 2 class teacher, anticipating her maternity break in April 2014 and her transition arrangements. She had already informed the class as well.

Just a couple of days before this email arrived in my inbox, my daughter was asking me about how babies were born. "Do storks drop them like they show in the movie *Dumbo?*" I thought I was prepared for this conversation as I had read up and watched enough videos about the "Good Touch/Bad Touch" conversations with toddlers. Being a graduate in biology, I was confident that I would be able to answer any questions that my child would have. Oh boy! My over-confidence got me nailed!

While I did answer her first question with the fact that babies were delivered from the mother's womb, she immediately went on to ask if she was also born that way, and I affirmed. Her curiosity did not end there—she started venturing into territories that I was not fully prepared to respond to.

She wanted to know how the baby got into the mother's tummy in the first place. Would hugging or kissing a boy do that? I replied, "For babies to be born you need to be married and that marriage age is typically 18 years or older."

The email from the teacher required me to elaborate on this aspect. My heart was racing in anticipation of our evening connection ritual. My daughter did not start the conversation. So, I prompted with a question, "How was your day at school today? Was there something your teacher talked about with you?"

"My teacher announced the arrival of her baby." responded my daughter... After a moment's pause... "She is not married!"

I was in a country where nudity was a norm in sculptures and art pieces, and same-sex marriages and PACS relationships, the French equivalent to a civil partnership, were legal. I was living in the Western world where people were ahead in accepting and normalizing gender-based conversations, when the rest of the world was playing catch up. And if I wished to not shut my child out from talking to me, then it was time for me to work on my inhibitions, conditioning, and limitations, even if my opinions were not in line with what she was learning, experiencing, and aligning to.

"Oh... is that so? I know I kind of indicated that babies are born only after marriage, but that is not always true. Do you still want to know how babies are formed?" I was thinking through in my head how best I could express my thoughts without being judgmental.

Smack came the response, "I know how they are formed!"

Even as I write, I can still feel the momentary shock. There was no turning back! "Really? Can you tell me what you know?"

She went on to explain the fusing of sperm and egg inside the mother's uterus and that the cells start dividing to form an embryo. And yes, she used those specific terms. She also had a decently clear explanation of the various growth phases in the three trimesters till a baby was birthed.

"How did you find out so much? Did your teacher teach you this in class?"

"No, I saw it in a picture book in our library."

"Are you allowed to take books from any rack?" I asked, assuming she had taken a book that was in the section for high school students.

"No, there are designated racks for us to pick our books from. I can take it only from there and give it to our teacher for her to make a record of our reading activity during library period."

Now, I was curious to know how a second-grader-level book had such elaborate information. When I was in high school, even the reproductive system was never covered in such detail. I was curious to know what more she knew. I probed on, "Does the book tell you how the sperm and egg come together?"

"No."

"Did the book give you information on the process of how a baby comes out into the world?"

"No."

"Is there something that you want to ask or talk about any of the things that we just discussed?"

A little hesitantly she asked, "You said babies are born only after one is married... but..."

Now, I had to be very careful in choosing the right words to explain why I said what I said without making anybody or any culture seem as being in the wrong. I grew up in a culture where sex and children outside marriage were shunned and punished in many families.

I took a deep breath and started responding, "Babies can be born without marriage. The details about how they form are not something I am ready yet to share with you today, but as you grow older and if you still want this answer 4 to 5 years from now, maybe I can try and answer at that time. In India, where I was born and grew up, it is expected that a couple marries before they can become parents. The belief is that while one parent (almost always the mother) cares for the children and the family, working inside the home, the other parent becomes the breadwinner by working outside the home. That is exactly how our home also is. In our case, it was by choice that we decided to stick to the norms and not force. Your father was ready to stay back while I worked, but I chose to resign as I wanted to be a stay-at-home parent."

"Is it wrong to have a child without marriage?"

"I am not sure if I can answer that question directly with a yes or no, but I personally think that it is difficult to have a child and raise it well, without marriage in a country like India. The family's and community's support are what helps in bringing up a child without too much of a workload on just the parent(s). In India, when you have a child outside of marriage, this support is non-existent in many cases. Sometimes, when a child is born outside of marriage, the parenting responsibility ends up on only one parent. In our home, you see your father and I split the responsibilities of home and child management between the two of us. If both need to be done by the same person, then it becomes too much on that one person. What do you think?"

"Yes… Without any support it will be too difficult for that one adult to do it all."

Thus ended our first long conversation on babies, partners, and marriage.

Gender constructs, gender discrimination, gender fluidity, and anything in between were topics that I started learning and understanding. Along the way, I also became mindful of my conditioning and the resulting limitations. Identifying my comfort zone helped me verbalize my thoughts in a sensitive and compassionate way which also impacted my parenting styles that heavily relied on open communication. Seeing me change has been a huge influence on my children sharing their ideas on these topics openly with me for discussion or debate with no hesitations.

***

To get back to where I began this narrative, the first 6 months after our relocation back to India were spent helping our younger child understand that he did not have to lose himself to belong. But at the tender age of 7, the speed at which he adapted to belong was fast and not completely in line with what I would have liked for him.

When he hit the 10-year-old mark, I started thinking of the right time to introduce the topic of puberty and menstruation. The classroom discussions and comments on this topic had not seen any progressive change from when I was a teen. It was still a topic discussed in hushed terms and the spotting of clothes being mocked with insensitive jibes among classmates. I wanted my son to be aware of what puberty meant and how it was experienced for both boys and girls. I also wished to educate him on what menstruation meant and how every girl and woman experienced it differently.

This meant that I needed to be educated enough on this topic to be able to answer basic questions that might arise from a 10-year-old. This time, instead of going the online route, I decided to talk to my spouse to understand how he navigated his puberty. Being a biology graduate himself our conversation was like a peer-group sharing. With both of us geared with the necessary information, we decided that we would both take turns bringing up conversations on these topics when an opportunity presented itself. This also began the journey of my spouse becoming an involved father and advocating on these topics.

Both my children were informed and educated about safe and unsafe touch, right from the time when they started off as good and bad touch. As parents, while we navigated these territories that were never a point of discussion in many households in India (even to date), we started becoming more mindful of our own unconscious biases and started changing the way we behaved and interacted not only with them but with the rest of the world as well. My son was introduced to what puberty meant for boys and girls with the biological facts including the concepts of PMS (pre-menstrual symptoms) and related mood swings. My husband took the responsibility of discussing the more intimate details of the changes that a boy goes through in puberty; I too was geared up to answer any curiosity queries that might come our way.

I had a talk on menstruation, sanitary pads, their purpose, and the associated mood swings, pain, and energy drain. I told him that every girl and woman experiences this differently and that he must be sensitive by not joining hands with his friends when they crack jokes at menstruating girls. If and where possible, he could also be supportive by either making his friends aware of it or informing any trusted adult about mockery.

When he had questions about the third gender, we sat down together to try and answer them to our knowledge. When I noticed him joining his friends to annoy girls from his class or playground mates, I took the time to point out that this amounted to bullying. When he responded that the girls also annoyed boys, I had to tell him that one wrong behavior could not nullify another, even if it was in retaliation.

Now, with my son in his tweens and my daughter well into her teens, the discussions are a lot more interesting. We, the parents, are the learners, while our children help mentor and teach us the current trends in concepts and advocacy.

***

In a nutshell, here is what has helped us in nurturing our children to be gender sensitive:

- **Walk the talk:** Working on ourselves by becoming more self-aware of our conditioning and resultant unconscious bias.

- **Use inclusive language:** To do this, the first step is to learn and equip ourselves with words that are inclusive that can replace the existing usage such as man, woman, guys and girls, policeman, with people, children, police person or police personnel. Making sure that we can let go of a biased upbringing that prompts one to make statements such as "Don't cry like a girl" or "Man up."

- **Be a learner for life:** Be open to learning from every experience of our life, understand the world that our children are growing up in, thereby creating an open two-way communication channel, that is devoid of the traditional parental hierarchical model of information flow from top down.

- **Develop a growth mindset:** Be open to discussing and debating opposing points of view (POV) and accepting new ideas or ideals when the opportunity presents itself, even if it means learning from our children.

- **Set healthy boundaries:** Be able to clearly define boundaries, limitations, and challenges, conveying the same to our children while also giving them the space to do the same, instead of forcing our ideas and thoughts as the final authority.

- **Step out of comfort zone:** Seek out communities and groups that welcome people from diverse backgrounds and cultures (race, religion, country, language, sexuality); spend quality time understanding the differences and similarities, while appreciating the richness this diversity brings with it. Expose ourselves and our children to these differences in perspectives and enrich our individual and collective learning experiences.

- **Be involved:** Develop the habit of active listening, spending quality time with your children, and being receptive and accepting of their POV, even when it is something that is not personally agreeable, provided it is safe for them. Be present when they need you the most.

- **Unconditional love:** Nothing can outweigh unconditional love. Children have a right to have a POV different from their parents. This is even normal considering the fact that the world the children grow up in is completely different from that of the parents when they were children themselves. Accept these differences and the resulting perceptions and opinions that change because of this, instead of saying "My way or the highway."

This is how we, as parents, managed to break the cycle of conditioning, by being the change ourselves. In our journey thus far, what we found as a real pillar of strength was being part of groups and communities that had people with similar interests, willing to break the toxic patterns of the past and share and work toward the common goal of a better childhood experience for their children.

In our personal life, this learning journey as involved parents continues. We urge more parents to be ready to share their parenting stories with the rest of the world for everyone to benefit from. While every parenting journey is unique, having a community to fall back on and knowing that we are not alone in this, goes a long way in boosting our morale and strengthening our resolve to create new and better experiences!

Chapter 5

PARENTING THROUGH MY MENTAL HEALTH JOURNEY

Jenna Clancey

"Taking care of myself doesn't mean 'me first'. It means 'me too'."

—L.R. Knost

"I came up on the 'postpartum depression radar' again," I said to my husband after our daughter's 9-month pediatrician appointment. "They suggested journaling and if it gets worse to see a therapist."

Here goes. I opened my brand new, beautiful shiny pink journal and closed my eyes. My heart sped up and my hands started to sweat. "Breathe…" I began to write.

Day one, giving this a try… WTF is my problem?!?! I have everything I've asked for and I can't keep myself together.

My brain gets overwhelmed and I can't calm down and I spiral into a panic… WHY WON'T THIS BABY GO TO SLEEP!

How do I get her to eat normal foods? I forget to feed myself and when I do remember/make an effort I don't do any more than microwave some meals. I don't want her to have a complex about food and eating like I do—how do I model good, healthy eating behavior?

I'm so lonely because I feel like I can't share that I don't have it all together. I hold it together on the outside (I think?) and then completely lose it in private...

How do I fix this?

Being a mother is the only thing I have ever known I was supposed to be. Growing up, girls around me dreamed of jobs, vacations, their weddings. I dreamed about being a mom. I loved being around kids, participating in activities, and teaching them new skills. Even potty training did not scare me off! I found any and every excuse to work with kids, play with kids, or just be around them. I could not wait to be "the house" that all of the kids wanted to go to; the coolest (and healthiest) snacks, the best playroom, amazing activities, and a pool in the back. I was going to be the person that children went to when they needed advice, a "safe" grown-up outside of their parents that could help. I was going to have it all.

Looking back, I had no idea what I was in for. Yes, I had taken care of a child (even multiple children) for days on end when their adults went out of town. But I was always able to come back to my life. As an autonomous adult. With some control. But motherhood is different. It is constant. And unforgiving. And wonderful. And beautiful. And hard.

I was not prepared for the major shift that my body and my mind went through, from dreaming of being an amazing mom to feeling like I was barely getting by. The hypervigilance and sleepless nights despite the fact that the baby was safe and sleeping. The swirling thoughts and overplanning. The difficulty finding moments of joy. The loss of confidence in my instincts. I was in the throes of what I now know was postpartum anxiety and depression. And as it turns out, I had been battling anxiety my whole life.

So many parents, especially mothers, feel a sense of failure if they are not everything to everyone. Perfection, or the outward appearance of perfection, as the expectation for mothers, is unattainable. And dangerous. I now consider myself a recovering perfectionist. As person who has been striving for perfection for so long and is nourished by the times when it is achieved, embracing the inevitable messiness that is parenting has rocked my world.

The coping strategies that worked to calm my anxieties in the past were no longer enough and sometimes not even possible. A lot of what I used to do, and as it turns out needed to do, to keep myself level revolved around being autonomous. Making and keeping a schedule that was my own, or mine, and my significant others. Being able to step back from certain emotional and social responsibilities as needed. Sleep. Period. End of sentence.

As I stepped back from a traditional work environment and into a flexible one with my primary responsibility being motherhood and caretaking, the predictability and stability of my old life melted away. In my effort to be the "perfect" mother, the "best" mother, I completely lost myself. The person I was—the partner, friend, and woman—became an afterthought. I was afraid to let go of my dream of motherhood and merely accept my reality. My anxiety and depression were running the show instead of being a part of my story.

Before, I used to pride myself in being the one that could always get things done. Need something taken off your plate? I have got you. Need something done efficiently and correctly? I'm your girl. Need someone to make a plan and focus on all the details? I live for that. And after? Forgetting a water bottle on a trip to the park would send me into a spiral. My thoughts would take me to scary places—I forgot her water bottle so she is going to be thirsty, then she is going to have a tantrum, then she is going to work herself up so much that she is going to make herself sick, then she is going to get dehydrated, then I'm going to have to take her to the hospital, and the doctors are going to think I'm not giving her food and water and they will call the police, and then, and then, and then...

In an effort to prevent these thoughts, I would try to plan everything down to the minute:

- We are meeting friends at the park at 2:00 p.m. We need to leave by 1:40 p.m.
- That means I need to start putting shoes on at 1:30 p.m. so that we can get into the car at 1:35 p.m. and buckle in.
- That means I need to be ready by 1:25 p.m.
- That means I need to be out of the shower, dressed, have my makeup and hair done by 1:20 p.m.

And, the list would go on.

Inevitably, I would plan out the day so precisely and, I was so hyper-focused, that if I woke up at 6:00 a.m. to get everything started and looked over at my clock and it was 6:05 a.m., I was convinced I had ruined the whole day. And this brought on my anger and rage. My husband called it the "paper towel moment." I would bottle my anger and frustration until I could not contain it any longer and I would explode at something seemingly insignificant—like my husband forgetting to change the roll of paper towels. Hence the name. I did not know how to admit that I wanted, no, needed, help.

***

Day Something. Who even knows anymore.

Maybe I have such anxiety because I feel like I'm on my own with this... and I feel so guilty that I want and need time away from her. Most people would kill to be in the situation I'm in and here I am complaining about it. Am

I ungrateful? Selfish? Crazy? It's what I wanted—it's what I dreamed about my whole life. The only thing I've ever known I was supposed to do and here I am not able to do it… I love her… oh do I love her… but being a mom is SO hard. So much pressure, such high stakes and I'm terrified to fail. So much so that sometimes I feel paralyzed.

That was my last journal entry before seeking professional help.

When my daughter was 17 months old, I had my first conversation with a therapist. I have never looked back. I wish I could say that from the moment I started with a therapist everything moved in a forward direction, the "right" direction. It did not. There are still ups and downs, seasons of my life and parenthood that allowed me to feel some of my highest highs but also my lowest lows. One of the things that therapy has shown me is how to let go of the original plan of how I wanted my life to look in favor of a healthy and happy one. I realized that by trying to hold on to perfection I was not allowing happiness and joy in my current life. Not only did I not deserve that, my husband and daughter did not deserve that either. I have mourned my perfect life and come to a place of acceptance and understanding. While my life will look different than I thought, it will be a new version of fulfillment and joy. Everyone's version of "perfect" is different and now I enjoy perfect moments in my own day and my own life. They are there as long as I pause and look for them.

I think the most important thing that I learned in therapy was the value of rest. Not just physical rest, although that is important too. But mental and emotional rest. Taking a break from an activity that is causing stress. Allowing some of the less important daily tasks to be pushed off until tomorrow. Muting a social media account that triggers you. Prioritizing myself and allowing that to drive my decisions, including drawing healthy boundaries around things that do not suit me or my family. Admitting to myself that instead of another cup of coffee, I was allowed to go to bed and start fresh in the morning. Giving myself the same grace that I have always given to others.

I always equated "rest" with laziness. I thought that if I could, I should. To not take on a task, complete a chore, finish an assignment, or volunteer to help when I was capable of doing so was a failure, regardless of the effect on me. That, if someone was to see me resting, there was judgment about me as a person and as a mother. Through therapy, understanding that not only was I not being my best self by continuing to say yes and pushing through, but that I was actually missing out on a lot of the little everyday joys that come with motherhood. The stress and exhaustion were clouding the first smiles and laughs. The learning of new things. The singing and dancing to the music.

Rest is productive. It is a reset. A chance to breathe and regulate. Sometimes a chance to laugh and smile, sometimes a chance to remember that "this too shall pass."

I think one of the reasons it was so hard for me to internalize the value of rest was that I enjoyed being the one who could take care of everything and everyone. Part of my self-appointed identity as the helper was lost when I became a mother. The invisible work, the mental load, that came with parenthood became my biggest barrier. The so-called "little things"—making sure the baby was hitting milestones, doing research on teaching styles, making sure the correct size clothes were in the closet, a feeding plan, the scheduling, the planning—consumed me. I had worked jobs before with lots of moving parts, attention to detail, and demands. But now, the stakes never felt higher and I was convinced that any misstep or mistake would have dire consequences.

I felt such guilt that I had the exact life that I asked for but I could not do it all. I am incredibly privileged—I have a spouse to share the parenting load, we have more than enough with one salary, we do not have to think about where our next meal comes from, we have a roof over our heads in a wonderful and safe neighborhood, we have family and friends that we can rely on if we ever need anything—and yet, I felt such shame that I was falling apart. By comparison to most of the people around me, I had little that I actually "needed" to do and yet I could not keep up with it. I felt like I was failing.

Before becoming a mother, my anxiety outwardly presented itself as being over-prepared, a perfectionist, dependable, and people-pleasing. Qualities and characteristics that I have been praised for and leaned into my entire life. I could be in control, I could "plan for the unexpected." And when my insides were racing, I could hide from the chaos. Now, suddenly, on the inside, everything felt hard. Getting up in the morning felt hard. Brushing my teeth, getting things ready for the day, and feeding myself and my daughter. By the time something came up that was actually difficult—my daughter having an age-appropriate tantrum, loss of childcare for the day, sickness in the family—I was past exhaustion and past my breaking point.

***

Shortly after my daughter turned two, I began medication to treat depression and my general anxiety disorder. As my doctor put it, "The meds won't take away the anxiety; they just smooth out the pointy edges." From the moment I held the pill bottle in my hands, I felt like I could finally breathe. There was a hope that with the tools that I learned—and would continue to practice—in therapy and "smoother edges," I would start to feel like myself again. The hypervigilance and intrusive thoughts are now fewer and farther between. The hard parts of my day are manageable and I find strength in working through them instead of despair. I have allowed myself to be vulnerable and trust that my perfection is not what defines me.

As I come up on almost two years of taking medicine, I can honestly say that I'm feeling more like myself. A different, imperfect, more accepting version of myself, but I think that is the beauty of parenthood. You are never the same. The only hope is that you can adjust to your new normal and still find a way to be yourself. Be a mother, a spouse, a friend and daughter. Take deep breaths and pauses when needed but know that when one has a "paper towel moment" (because, let us face it, it will still happen) that it is all right. It is not failure, it is being human.

I have rediscovered the passion that I once had to allow me to find things that bring me joy. Time and reflection have allowed me to see some of the beautiful things about my journey. Now I can be truly honest about my struggles, and because of that, I have formed an amazing village around me. The ones that have been a part of my highest highs and picked me up after my lowest lows. No questions. No judgments. The mamas, the friends, the support system that sees the real me. Not for my perfect house or perfect snacks or perfect activities (although my activity packs are fabulous). The ones that are just there beside you, wiping your child's nose when it runs, sending the check-in text, pouring you a drink at your own house, or dropping off a coffee when they know you have had a long week. The village that helps make me the best version of myself, and I can only hope that they feel the same way.

***

In the 165th episode of her podcast *We Can Do Hard Things*, author and podcaster Glennon Doyle shares about her struggle with a new eating disorder diagnosis.[1] Something she said resonates with every fiber of my being. Paraphrasing, she said that she was very unsure about picking this time to open up about her struggle because she was "still in the messiness of it" but she could not be her authentic self without this part of her story. I too find that I am only comfortable showing vulnerability when I have come out the other side. Found a solution. Wrapped everything up in a tidy little bow.

I am hoping that by sharing my journey as I am living it, it will help others who are struggling and perhaps suffering in silence. Things have changed so much for our generation and the way motherhood is presented, especially on the internet, has had such a tremendous impact on our generation of parents. We see a highlight reel of perfectly curated moments that portray a false sense of parenthood. I'm now able to look at those photos and see the behind-the-scenes that everyone goes through despite what they chose to share. The inherent messiness that we are all going through as we create our own stories.

I think the fact that I am slightly terrified to share my story of parenting and mental health screams how important it is. Despite my struggles, I liked the idea that to most people I still "had it all together." I do not. And I never will, and that is ok. And if no one has shared with you that no one has it all together, everyone is just doing their best, let me be the first. But hopefully not the last.

NOTES

1. "Glennon's Diagnosis & What's Next," *We Can Do Hard Things: The Podcast*, January 3, 2023.

Chapter 6

PARENTING IS ABOUT BEING THE BEST VERSION OF YOURSELF

Anjna Parameswaran

"Life is about accepting the challenges along the way, choosing to keep moving forward and savouring the journey."

—Roy T. Bennet

When does one really become a parent? To some the feeling of being a parent arrives as early as they conceive, to others only after they have held their fragile baby in their hands does the feeling of having become a parent rush in. To me, it has been a continuous process—from the day I conceived till this very day!

Motherhood has been a long road, and an adventurous joyride. I have been a worried parent, constantly fretting about the choices that I made for my daughter and then worried about the ones that she made or might in the future. During my "worrying phase," I somehow forgot to enjoy the process of her growing up and becoming an awe-inspiring individual in herself. Now, it is as if I have been in the abyss and finally, I am arriving. In that spirit, this chapter is not about the dos and don'ts of parenting but about enjoying each moment of this journey that we consciously choose to undertake. Throughout, I will share some of the lessons I have learned about myself along the way.

***

Once, someone I know was at a supermarket and saw this young toddler wreaking havoc. She was running around, screaming, shouting, demanding practically everything she could touch while her mother refused to comply.

Everyone was looking at this uncontrollable child and judging the mother for her failure. When the mother reached the billing counter with none of the things the toddler had demanded, the child went into a rage and began crying at the top of her voice. The mother, who was now right behind my friend in the line, was surrounded by piercing gazes from all the customers and super-market staff.

Then, the mother loudly started saying, "Meera, calm down. Meera, relax." She reiterated these words several times before being interrupted by the lady behind her in the queue who said, "Excuse me, but I don't think your plea to calm Meera down is working." At this, the mother smiled at my friend, at the cashier, and at the lady who had just spoken and very calmly said, "I am Meera. I am calm enough to not lose my composure at the behavior of a child."

While I cannot speak to what the lady thought to Meera's reply, I must tell you after hearing about this encounter I was very impressed because if it had been me, I would have expected a 3-year-old to be self-controlled, well-behaved, polite, and respectful instead of being a 3-year-old! I was inspired by Meera's self-awareness and ability to distance herself from the judgment and assumptions of others. To keep going and stay focused on the person she wished to be in that moment with her daughter. I have reflected many times on this story and its lessons since.

***

When I became a mother and the responsibility of raising a human being dawned upon me, I thought hard and deep. For the first few months, I struggled to even adjust my child to the world outside my belly and then I struggled to get her adjusted to a normal sleeping pattern. When I finally got used to all this, I struggled to get her to be in somebody else's lap for more than 10 minutes at a stretch for she refused to let go of me. Each night I cradled her in my arms to sleep, and I wondered what I would do next. I felt my energy draining and my patience dwindling. I felt like screaming, shouting, crying, and blaming everyone for this mess that I had got myself into.

At such a time of emotional sensitivity, I thought about that mother who did not let go of her composure in the supermarket. Taking a cue from this incident, I asked myself, *did I want to raise my child with childish impatience or childlike joyfulness?*

Yet being joyful every second of every minute is a trying and tiring task, even for the most patient of all beings, irrespective of our choosing to be the ideal parent at every step of the way. This rollercoaster of a ride is filled with adrenaline, ups and downs, twists and turns, and lots of mess to clear up on the way. Although I am not a perfectionist, I have certain ideals that I swear by and when my daughter took my life through a fragrant storm, I saw all my rules, regulations, and deliberations get swept away with the tide of her never-ending glee and energy.

As she began to gain her own personality, I understood that we are two different people even though she is a part of me and I of her; her individuality is unique, intriguing, and challenging. It took me time to accept this difference and thereby accept the fact that her approach to life and daily activities is going to be very different from mine. I now have learned to agree that even though the apple does not fall far from the tree, no two apples on that tree will taste exactly alike.

***

I remember meeting this exceptionally gifted 6-year-old who could read like a pro. This child was undoubtedly impressive, and I loved how involved her parents were in ensuring their child strives forever to achieve brilliance. They would engage her in reading varied texts and play enticing reading games with her. Extremely motivated, I decided to follow in their footsteps with my 3-year-old and got her fancy reading material as well as activities.

And so, we sat down with the first book that she chose and read along poetically. We sang, we laughed, and we had fun! I noticed, though, that she did not really learn much through it. For her it was more about our giggles, rolling around on the floor, singing along, and so on. For me, it was more about her learning a skill and not so much about the experience. The situation infuriated me, and I flew into a silent rage, questioning my ability to train my child and her ability to excel in life! In my ambitious parenting, I lost priceless time.

I wish I had learned from that one mistake but sadly I did not. A fool of habit, I take my sweet time to learn and adapt. Aspiring constantly to make my child competent enough to show off to the world, I keenly kept introducing popular fads in training toddlers, ignoring that her interests and curiosities might be different from her peers (around the world).

I remember dunking her in the children's pool at a young age, even though I am myself a terrible swimmer. She fretted for her life, scared of the water until she turned six. When I saw her cousin swimming like a fish, I felt that I was not doing enough to motivate my child into being the best version of herself and I questioned where I was going wrong. It took me a good span of time to appreciate the fact that I had to let her discover herself on her own and all that I could do in the meantime was to support her through her journey of self-discovery. Over-imposing myself upon a young child was not only creating a pressure cooker situation for her at home, but it was equally detrimental to my mental peace and composure. I had entered the "typical Indian parent zone," even though I had wanted to be a responsive parent!

Many times, I have caught myself comparing my 7-year-old to myself when I was that age, and honestly, I do not remember how I was at that time. I assume that I was more obedient, responsible, and dedicated as a youngster and expect my apple to be my exact replica. I stopped myself from telling her that I used to always respect my parents' hard work and value money and dedicated myself to studies as we belonged to a middle-class immigrant family in Delhi. In my approach to teaching her through example, I tried giving her my own example from a different age and time which would be completely unrelatable to her. My child, born and raised in the era of technology, worldwide exposure, Netflix, and more would face a varied set of struggles that would be nothing like that of mine. What I then started to solve was how to prepare her for new-age challenges.

***

My daughter's seventh birthday taught me a valuable lesson in parenting. This was the first time I was organizing a big party without my husband around and the thought of dealing with 25 children of my daughter's age group gave me shivers. I wanted it to be perfect the way most other parties were; with perfect decor, food, cake, games, and return gifts—which is such a rage these days! My elderly, yet extremely energetic and enthusiastic parents, offered to extend whatever help I needed, yet somehow the pressure of having everything perfect kept me up most nights of the week before the party. No matter how much I tried to convince myself that it was just a party for a 7-year-old, I could not keep my nerves calm.

Anyway, I got ready with the theme—all pink and pretty, something I assumed she wanted. I started arranging and micromanaging, losing my mind over small little details. I did not want to use balloons and other items of waste because I just could not see the point of contributing to the ever-growing landfills. I needed eco-friendly alternatives and most importantly to keep a cool head about everything.

I tried keeping my daughter in the loop on decision-making so that she would feel involved and appreciate the tedious task of planning a party. She would happily listen to everything that I had to say and eventually finish my soliloquy with a "But I want it all, Ma." I saw my preferences overcome by her wants as I desperately tried to get all that was needed to arrange the perfect Pink Party.

No matter how hard I tried I could not find an alternative to balloons.

Finally, the day arrived, when all she could think about were the gifts, cake, and games with her friends while I got nervous about making sure that everything went smoothly. Her friends came, they danced, they played, they sang and had a lot of fun.

To them, the party was about "fun," nothing more, nothing less. They wanted to smile, laugh, and enjoy—something that all adults want too—but our joy gets lost in translation. I had failed to read between the lines when my daughter had said—"But I want it all, Ma." All I needed to do as a parent was to take the time to understand what she really wanted instead of what I wanted to provide for her. Raising my child is more about her than about me, and so, I had to resolve that as well as providing her with memorable experiences in life, I also needed to offer a safe space where she felt at liberty to express her true desires and needs.

***

When I began this journey of being a parent to my darling Juno, I had forgotten completely that my child was the most organic thing that nature had bestowed upon me. I did not need to take any classes or rely upon unsolicited advice to do something that nature had created me for. All I had to do was just go with it.

However, as the world is a daunting place, I began aspiring to mimic popular trends in parenting instead of following the natural footprints engraved by my mother before me and her mother before her. I was mesmerized by the accessible tips on parenting available for a negligible amount almost wherever I stopped. It was like the whole world had started recognizing the pattern of my interest and broadcasting before me the things that I thought I wanted but never really needed. Peer pressure has a strange way of making its path into our minds!

Over time, I have realized that all I really need to do is to take a few breaths and then get on to figuring out what my child desires and where I can best support. An objective approach, which helps me in my professional life, was the way to go in my personal life too and has helped me in being a loving and responsive parent to my child. By being supportive I do not enable her to feed her fears and weaknesses; rather, I help her to accept her strengths and traverse her fears, just like I do for myself when I am faced with a challenging situation at work.

As an individual, my daughter will create a path for herself eventually and learn all that is important for her to thrive in the world—confidently navigating any bumps in the road she may face along the way. All I want for her is to hug me and pour her heart out to me whenever she feels like it and even though I might not be able to snatch away all her pains and struggles, I believe my warmth will strengthen her to express herself freely and eventually overcome any problem in life. Something that my mother has always done for me.

My mother has always lent a patient ear, provided unbiased opinions whenever asked for, and cheered for me loudly whenever I stumbled, to help me lift myself up without ever doing it for me. My parents have always let me make my decisions, my mistakes, and my discoveries and imbibe my own learnings without ever influencing my life with their teachings. Their presence has hovered upon me like a friendly cloud and from that, I have derived considerable confidence. To them I owe much and from them, I gather the inspiration to raise my child.

***

Parenthood has not only been about me raising my daughter but has also been about me raising myself along with her. Adjusting to her preferences, accepting her sporadic personality, and creating a more comfortable space for her to feel wonderful about herself rather than baby-proofing the house, choosing children-friendly places to go to, or deciding to settle at a location that has a good school and friendly neighborhood.

Most of my friends tell me that they learned to be more patient after their baby was born; they sacrificed their hopes and aspirations to raise their baby well. This has not been true for me. I continued studying during my pregnancy because I had to take a break from work due to a low-lying placenta which demanded some amount of bed rest. After she was born, I automatically adjusted to her sleep pattern, which was erratic and insufficient, yet my mother's assistance enabled me to finish a post-graduate degree and a teacher's training course.

Somehow, after she was born, I found myself always more driven to be the best version of myself and kept working hard to achieve more financial and emotional independence. As my husband has a transferable job, we were able to provide a rich cultural and travel experience to her until she turned six and both of us wanted some stability for her. That is when I decided to get out of my comfort zone of being in a protective environment and move out into a strange city with my little one. She has somehow been a propelling force for me to charge into the world with more energy and power than I ever knew I possessed.

Much like my own parents, she is constantly the wind beneath my wings, and this was something I discovered as soon as I held her close to my heart. To her, I am the definition of her world, and that in itself is empowering. I wish for her to see the same spark of love, excitement, faith, and belief in my eyes for her that I see in her eyes for me. In her innocence lies deep wisdom that I have learned to imbibe slowly yet fully.

There have been times when I have tried controlling her actions and words in the assumption that I know the best and that only I can steer her toward the correct direction. My expectations of my child sometimes are unbelievably unrealistic and whenever I rationalize them, I understand how silly I had been. Appreciating her individuality and celebrating her unique traits is all that I can do as a mother, allowing her to blossom into her perfect self rather than fitting into my expectation. When I know that I can only be happy being myself, doing what I enjoy, and exploring the world through my experiences, then it make sense that I should allow her too to fall and get up, live and learn the ways to her joys, discover her own talents and work toward honing them because eventually she, just like me, deserves to lead a happy and content life of her own choosing.

***

For my child to rely on me, I have realized that I need to be reliable. Without bursting into fits of rage or even a slight expression of disappointment on my face when she does something I do not really approve of. As adults, we frown upon being judged and stay wary of people who judge us for various reasons that we do not even know of. And so, the thing that works best in my household is to keep judgments out like dirty shoes. It does not mean that I do not enforce corrective measures or point out something unbecoming of a gentle person in my child. I just aspire to do it carefully and with the bigger picture in my mind.

One day my daughter came home and sadly declared that her friends had smashed an injured chameleon to death because it looked scary and unappealing. I could see that she had not willingly participated in the act and even though I was horrified at the cruelty committed, I had to consciously take a minute to recollect my emotional balance and address this situation rationally. I understand that peer pressure is a daunting reality and as adults we sometimes find it difficult to empathize with children who succumb to it, but I knew in that moment this incident was just the first of many such accidents that might follow if my daughter does not learn to confidently deal with a tough situation. After all, her decisions in life are going to be her own and the consequence of each of them shall have to be endured by her on her own. Yet, as a mother, I had to at least shine light upon the path that she can take without influencing her decisions.

So, I asked her to revisit the event, which was rather uncomfortable for her, and very reluctantly she did it. Immediately afterwards, she looked at me and said that she could have refused to be a spectator even if she could not have stopped the others from doing what they did. Enabling her to own the choice she made that day and then, without judgment, explore different options she might choose next time, made her feel more confident about establishing a stand without really losing the favor of her peers.

When I told my husband about it, he was rather calm and did not react at all. He told me that she was just a child and that she would learn the ways of the world on her own, but he did not dismiss what I had done, nor did he question what she had done. Although our techniques of parenting differ sometimes, we both look forward to the same end result and that has really helped me discover the joys of parenting.

***

My husband and I have discussed having another baby because we have been told plenty of times that eventually, our only daughter will get lonely without a sibling. We are advised that having a sibling during childhood is necessary for lasting memories; with a sibling, a child learns to share, care, love, and nurture.

Sometimes, I do agree with all these reasons to have another baby because I have an elder brother and when I look back into my growing-up years, I cannot imagine anything going well if it was not for him. He introduced me to the best things in life that I cherish even now such as books and music. In fact, he is the one who got me my first pet cat when I was 11 years of age and since then my life changed for the better. Animals became an integral part of all our lives and ever since we have not lived a day without being surrounded by animals. My brother has always been there for me whenever I needed him and even after he moved to another country for work, he made sure that his presence did not diminish from my life. When I think about my relationship with my brother, I yearn for Juno to have the same with her own sibling.

However, when I talk to the most rational influence in my life, that is my husband, he carefully points out that the world has changed so much and with it, the relationships that people cherished have changed as well. People have become more self-reliant and independent and are not afraid of seeking emotional support from a professional, in case of a need. With the newer generation, I can see that the meaning of friendship has a deeper value, and the internet has made it possible for them to stay in touch with each other irrespective of boundaries. My daughter is very enterprising and manages to keep herself engaged. She makes friends easily and loves socializing with her peers. She is happy in her own way and that is something I as a mother should cherish, instead of worrying about something that might or might not happen. Just because I had something does not mean that she needs to have the same thing. Life would be meaningful for her irrespective of similar shared experiences.

***

I feel I am growing up with my daughter through each experience that we share and encounter. I do not equate this feeling with aging, because I do not think that parenting is a mundane drudgery. In fact, it is more like an unexpected gift with something new each time you open a layer of wrapping paper. Through this course of time, I have learned to not throw a tantrum when I cannot control my daughter's tantrum which would only make me lose a piece of my mind and render me vulnerable. I have learned that a child will behave like a child, but I can choose to behave like a grown-up, making better choices emotionally and physically without being driven by my impulses.

My daughter has taught me to cherish the smallest things that happen around us and enjoy the moment at hand without overthinking about the future. After all, she will only be little for a very short amount of time, and the majority of her life she will spend as an adult, so why should not I make better use of this wonderful time that I have with her? There is so much for us to do together which might not necessarily involve a prominent teaching and learning experience but may have a deeper impact on her mind.

I have decided to value each time that I get to hug her, kiss her, and hold her closer to myself over anything else for the time being, and just like judgments and dirty shoes, I shall leave work stress and my idle sense of perfection outside the door. I may not stop micromanaging, for that is a tough habit to get rid of, but then parenting is not about changing one's personality to accommodate the personality of your child. It is more about finding out what works best in the given space and time without creating any agitation or tension.

In the words of Kahlil Gibran, "Your children are not your children. They are sons and daughters of Life's longing for itself. They come through you but not from you. And though they are with you, yet they belong not to you. For they have their own thoughts." His words have served as a constant reminder for me every time I start personalizing my relationship with my daughter to such an extent that I become obsessed with her and her actions. This has only enabled me to appreciate that she is an individual and the creator of her life.

Chapter 7

LEARNING TO FEEL, PROCESS, AND SUPPORT EMOTIONS AS A PARENT

Denise Varughese

"Because we all want to see our children as good kids, see ourselves as good parents, and work toward a more peaceful home. And every one of those things is possible. We don't have to choose. We can have it all."

—Dr. Becky Kennedy

It was one of those mornings with preschoolers where time moves slowly even though the clock is speeding by.

We had done the morning routine—potty, teeth, banana and peanut butter and toast and milk, dress, hair, find matching socks (fail), and look for shoes that are never where they are supposed to be.

But then, they would not get in the car.

"Get in the car."

"No."

"Get. In. The. Car."

"I don't want to go to school."

I felt the heaviness settle on top of my chest, and push down on my shoulders. The anger and anxiety pushed up my throat. We had been here so many times before.

I took a breath. I can be calm.

"Get in the car and then when we get home later, we can play a game."

"No."

I stared at them. They stared at me.

"If you don't get in the car right now, you are going to lose your rainbow tutu."

"It's okay. I have my pink tutu."

I stared at them. They stared at me.

"I'm going to wait here. When you are ready let me know."

I sat in the front seat scrolling on my phone. They stood outside the car. Ten minutes passed. I was now entering "be late for work" territory.

I got out of the car and picked them up. If you have ever attempted this, you will know that putting an unwilling child in a car seat is a losing battle.

They thrashed, kicked. When I got one arm in, it came back out as I tried to get the other one through. Were they laughing at me?

I felt the buzz move up my throat and into my brain. It was like a match; it lit my brain on fire with frustration. If I keep struggling, I am going to hurt them, I thought. I let them go. I removed the top half of my body from the car. They slid to the floor of the back seat.

"Get in the car!"

I screamed it. The whole neighborhood heard. I am a terrible mother.

They did not move.

I sat in the front seat for a few more minutes. Silence from the backseat.

"Well, I'm going to work," I said.

I got in the car and started it. I was going to pull down the driveway to try and scare them into the seat.

"No!" they screamed. "No, no, no!"

I got to the edge of the driveway. They were still on the floor.

"Please get in your seat."

"No."

I waited in silence. We had been at this for nearly 30 minutes.

I drove back up the driveway. I parked the car in the garage and got out. I walked inside the house and sat on the couch. I started crying.

I was powerless. It was 8:30 a.m. and I was exhausted. I had no way to get this child to do what I needed them to do.

I tried offering a reward. I tried taking something away. I tried forcing them into the seat. I tried yelling. I tried scaring them. When I was their age, I just did what I was told, and on the rare occasion when I did not, my parents yelled and then I did what I was told. Why will my kid not do the same? I do not know what else to do to get this child into the car.

I do not remember how long I sat there. I checked on them a couple of times and when I came out the last time, they were sitting in the car seat. I went to buckle them and realized they had peed in the seat.

I remember thinking, did this child spite pee me?

I drove them to school. When we entered their preschool classroom, they announced, "I peed in my car seat," like it was an accomplishment, and then went to the in-room bathroom to change. The teacher took their things, told me they had it, and bless them, allowed me to leave.

The only thing that saved my sanity that morning was, when I finally arrived at work, two hours late, my coworkers (all women, many mothers) greeted me with hugs and validation. Parenting is the wildest of rides.

***

As a child, when I went to my mother with a problem, with an illness, with a scratch or a scrape, she would look at it, at me, and say, "Ya fine." It became a running joke. We never missed a day of school. We did not cry. We tried not to feel sad, or at least not to show it.

It was not an explicit thing. I do not remember either of my parents saying, "Don't cry" or "Don't be sad." I do not think we talked about it at all. They did not grow up that way; they did not know anything else.

I also learned that feelings were not meant to be felt because of my younger brother. He was a big-feeling kind of kid. I say this using the language I know now. Back then he was just labeled as "trouble"—the one most likely to throw a tantrum, and the class clown; the gregarious one who made everyone laugh, the one we walked on eggshells around so as not to trigger an eruption. I saw how hard it was for him. I saw how his big feelings caused a negative reaction. Seeing all of this, I think I chose to make my feelings private and small.

Now, 38 years old and the parent of three young children, I have finally started to learn how to talk about my feelings, communicate what I need, and unpack a lifetime of people-pleasing and pressing down emotions.

And you want me to parent like that, too? This is asking too much. How do you parent in a way you were not parented? How do you do it while you are still in process, still recovering, still untangling a childhood that gave way to an adulthood of gaps? How do you connect with a child and teach them to connect with themselves when you are still searching for yourself?

I know now that the yelling, the negotiating, the waiting, and the forcing does not work for me or my children. I have bought into the "gentle" parenting of influencers on Instagram and I read *Good Inside* by Dr. Becky Kennedy. I thought it was a warm hug. 10/10. Recommend. I want to be emotionally regulated and model that regulation for my children. I want to support them by naming and normalizing all feelings. I want to hold a curious stance and seek to understand what is under my children's behavior so they can learn to be curious about this for themselves. These things feel right to me; I have seen them work. But it still feels like I am playing a very, very long game. I know this way is better for me and my kids, and yet it still feels exhausting.

***

There is absolutely nothing that enrages me more as a parent than repeating myself over and over into the void because no one listens to me. Or rather, they hear me, but they do not follow my direction. This is at its worst at bedtime, when my introverted self is done with the day and ready to go into quiet mode to refuel.

"Okay, lovies, I'm setting the timer for 5 minutes. When the timer goes off, it will be time to put away the paper and scissors, and go upstairs."

Silence.

"Did you hear me?"

"Yeah." "Yes." "Yes."

The timer goes off.

"It's time to get ready for bed! Put the scissors and paper away."

"But I not done with my project."

"I know. It feels hard to stop doing an activity. It's okay to feel frustrated. You still need to put the project away now. You can do it again in the morning before school. Do you want to put it on the table or in the art basket?"

Name the feeling. Offer choice. When they will not choose, then make the choice for them to hold the boundary. The cycle continues and continues. It takes a lot of energy. Most nights we reach a place where everyone is tucked in and the house quiet. Some nights it still ends with me yelling, "Get in your bed and do not come out. I am tired and going to bed. Do not call me!" because we can try hard and still not be perfect.

***

In January of 2022, I reached out to my therapist, who I had not seen in 7 years, to see if she had capacity for another client. It had been a long two years: a twin pregnancy, a NICU stay for both babies, parental leave with two newborns, return to work outside the home and transition to daycare. And then, of course, the fall out of March 2020: working outside-the-home-full-time-jobs remotely alongside my partner, while sharing childcare for two infants and a 4-year-old. In August 2020 a layoff turned me into the full-time workday parent, as well as the virtual kindergarten facilitator. I returned to full-time work outside the home in the summer of 2021 and all my children returned to school and daycare. I was grateful that our family had safely navigated the beginning of the pandemic. And I was exhausted. I had existed in survival mode for so long.

I shared all of this with my therapist at our first session, and when I finally reached a pause, my therapist let the silence hang for a beat and then asked, "Denise, what do you want?"

I breathed in and opened my mouth. And nothing came out. I laughed because I had learned to name my children's feelings like a pro, but I did not know what I felt or wanted.

Over the next year, I explored this question. I also considered the deeper reasons for why I did not have an answer. I was a people-pleaser, I knew that. I felt my body clench at the thought of conflict; it was so much easier—more comfortable—to make sure everyone around me had what they wanted and needed before me. For the first time, I was able to name my tendency to over-function. I believed it was my responsibility to do it all. I grew up in a family where other people had needs that I viewed as bigger than mine, and so I put my head down and quietly paved my own path that did not require any support.

But what I had learned in childhood and spent a lifetime doing was not working anymore. It also was not necessary. I now had a home and a relationship where there was room for my needs. I could figure out what I wanted and say it out loud and know that my partner would hear it and we could work together to figure out how to make it happen. I did not have to grind quietly through life in an over-functioner's anxiety spiral.

***

It is a Saturday night and we have a babysitter coming. It is time to clean up and get ready for dinner. I have given my children a heads-up that it is almost time to stop playing and come to dinner. The timer goes off. One child does not want to stop working on the ocean floor puzzle.

"I not coming," they said. They sat up and crossed their arms.

"It looks like you are feeling mad."

"Don't talk to me!" They screamed and threw the box full of puzzle pieces across the room.

I wanted to scream back, "Are you kidding me? That puzzle is going in the garbage now."

I paused. I wondered if it was really about the puzzle.

"It seems like you are feeling mad right now and that's okay. It's not okay to throw things. What are you feeling in your body right now?" I asked.

"Don't talk to me!" they screamed again.

"Okay. I'm going to go to the next room and I will come back in a minute to check on you," I said.

I left the room. A minute later, I returned.

"Can you share what you are feeling in your body now?"

"I don't want you to go out. I don't want Miss Courtney to come."

I pause again.

"I see. So, you are feeling upset because you don't want Mommy and Daddy to leave. That's why you didn't come to dinner and you threw the puzzle."

"Yes."

I validate the feeling and name how we are still going to go out and then we will come back. We talk about what we can do together to help them feel better about Mommy and Daddy leaving. They decide that having their stuffed animal and playing the Gabby's Dollhouse game with Miss Courtney will help. We get the stuffed animal and pull out the game so it is ready. I text Miss Courtney to let her know my child is excited to play this game with her. Most of the time, it really does end like this. Some of the time it still ends with dinner refused and screaming as we walk out the door because we can all try hard and still not be perfect.

***

Throughout my life, and especially during the early pandemic years, I have used food as comfort. I had not felt like my body was my own for a while due to pregnancy and the emotional eating was not helping. When I looked in the mirror, I was the same person, but sometimes when I saw a picture of myself, I did not immediately recognize me as me. I had tried different approaches to addressing my eating habits, but all of them were weight loss and deprivation focused and they just did not work for me. I got connected with a registered dietitian who offers nutrition therapy and in one of our first sessions, as I described my need for comfort food, she advised that, when I feel that urge come on, I should pause and ask myself, "What is my unmet need right now?"

I had never thought to ask myself this question so explicitly, in real-time, and to honor the answer. I realized that when I finally got my three children down for nap and quiet time on a weekend afternoon, and I felt the urge to pull out the random things in the pantry and eat them while watching *Grey's Anatomy*, it was not because I really wanted the stale popcorn. I was overstimulated after a morning of kid activities and constantly meeting other people's needs. I needed quiet and release from providing anything to anyone. I could meet this need more effectively through a nap or a walk with my dog and a good audiobook. This is what I really needed. I was stopping to be curious about my children's behavior, so why could not I stop and be curious about my own?

I tested this question again and again—"What is my unmet need right now?" When I was feeling like I could not breathe and everything was spiraling out of control because the little kids had been sick at home for a week—I did not need to order a big lunch from Chipotle. My unmet need was time for myself and release from responsibilities that were not a priority. I needed to clear my calendar the best I could, put the kids in front of the TV, sip my hot coffee, and read for an hour. At bedtime, when my 7-year-old refused to stop an art project, and my twin 3-year-olds were screaming because one wanted an Elsa band aid (and, not an Anna band aid), and one could not find her puppy stuffed animal—and despite 20 minutes of asking them to come upstairs and waiting at the bottom of the stairs and eventually yelling and feeling like I am going to explode into five million pieces that will silently float to the floor of my home—I do not need to push through and have a big bowl of ice cream in the eventual silence. I need to tell my children I am taking a 5-minute break, go upstairs by myself (after ensuring they are safe), close my eyes and breathe in the silence, and then go back and try again.

***

Parenting is a very, very long game. I am consistently working on it. I know it will not ever feel "done" but some things will become easier.

Until then, I continue to go to therapy for myself, to build the internal muscle to acknowledge my feelings and needs. I also communicate with my partner to build the time to care for my needs so I can be regulated and model responding in a healthy way when I am dysregulated.

I think about how my child and I prepared for a recent doctor's appointment. They would be having a procedure they had never had before in a doctor's office they had never been to before. I called the provider and, though I felt like a burden, I asked them to walk me through what would happen at the appointment, step by step, so I could relay all the information to my child. We talked about it days before the appointment so my child would have time to process and ask questions and chip away at the anxiety they might feel. In the moment, I validated that it was okay to feel scared, it was okay to cry, and that they would still go through it to keep their body safe and healthy. I held their hand. I advocated for them to have time to ask questions. And when it was all over and we walked to the car, they turned to me and said, "It's okay that I cried. I felt really brave. I'm proud of myself."

I think about this sibling interaction I overheard recently. One child was sweeping with a play broom. The other took the broom out of their hands. The first child said, "No! I was using that." I peeked up from behind the book I was reading on the couch, bracing myself for the screaming and the hitting. The first child said, "I feel frustrated at you." The second child paused their sweeping. They handed the broom back to the first child. The first child said, "I can share. I go, then you go."

Raising children is truly the work of a lifetime, and perhaps even two lifetimes—for both you and your children. It spans eternity, really, as one generation learns and grows from the one before it. For me, as I attempt to reconnect with myself, while simultaneously providing a model to my children for how to connect with themselves, it has been wild. Many, many big feelings—for all of us. But we do it together every day, and when it does not work quite right, we take a break and try again. I know I do it alongside so many other parents living a similar experience, too.

I imagine us, sometimes; each in our own space, working to know ourselves, pulling encouragement from each other to fuel the growth of truth, connectedness, and joy in our homes. This bubble of warmth envelopes our children. It is giving them superpowers; I know it is. I imagine the adults we are becoming and the adults our children will become. What a beautiful community we will be. What a beautiful community we are.

Chapter 8

RAISING A CHILD AS A SINGLE PARENT

Preetha Bhaskar

"I'm a single mother by choice. One parent can be better than two."
—Katy Chatel

My journey of parenting started when I had no clarity as to where the journey of life was taking me. I never expected to be wearing the hat of both parents when I stepped into the role of a parent, having to hustle between work and life. This was extremely hard in the initial years of bringing up a child. I was unprepared when life's curveball hit me.

I was left in a circumstance where I did not have the privilege to choose between my career and being a parent. My spouse was non-existent in the parenting arena, and I was grappling to come to terms with that fact. No, we were not yet divorced when my child was born. This meant I had to be financially stable to care for my newborn child, while also learning the ropes of parenthood. This struggle to bring a balance between the roles of a new mother and the demands of a full-time job outside the home negatively impacted my parental connection time with my growing child.

My full-time job left me with hardly one to two hours a day with my child, and this was also possible because I was living with my parents, who lifted the weight of home chores from my head. The frustration of not being able to stay longer with my child and enjoy every precious moment during the initial rapid developmental years (0–3 years), the self-pity on my failed marriage, and by extension my life, pushed me into a depressive state and I withdrew from everything and everyone around me.

***

Being a single parent in India was personally a stressful state to be, as I was under extreme duress to be the best parent, thereby overcompensating for the lack of the other parent (father) in my son's life. I did not have a peer to consult with while having to make the most important decisions in my child's life. I did not have a peer to fall back on for the emotional and mental support of bringing up a child. I did not have a partner to brainstorm ideas for any parenting challenges that I faced while caring for my child. This made it emotionally draining. The fear of judgment from a patriarchal society, that a child brought up without a father would lack in manners or discipline, drove me to become that parent who was extremely critical of childish mistakes and pranks. There were lots of instances when I yelled as well as hit him for even the slightest, silliest mistakes any child his age would make. I was driven to perfecting him so that the world would not have the chance to find faults with him or me.

It took me a long time to realize that I had failed to see life and the world from his perspective. I was so focused on wanting to be the perfect parent who managed, that I never saw how I was negatively affecting my child's holistic development. This resulted in my son becoming aggressive and hyperactive outside the home. He started acting out in school.

I grew up with the social conditioning that when discipline did not work, then gift the child to do your bidding. So, from yelling and physical punishments, I went to the other extreme where I was now catering to every wish in the hope to fix his aggression and hyperactive behavior. This was also overdone as a gesture to compensate for my physical absence in my son's life. Little did I realize that I was encouraging a sense of entitlement in my son, and unwillingness to accept "No" as a valid response to any unrealistic or unjustifiable demands.

***

From the time of my son's birth, my spouse was unavailable. While the reasons are something I prefer to keep private, he never visited to see his son even after I informed him of the birth. So, from then on, we were separated and I moved in with my parents, with my brother and his family also supporting me and my parents caring for my son.

I am grateful to my parents and my brother for being the pillar of support that they were during those initial years of child development. Without them, I do not think my son would have been able to overcome the gaps in my parenting and the lack of a father in his life, without long-term damage to his self-image. They were also instrumental in helping me overcome my pessimism and self-pity and look at life from a more opportunistic outlook. Here are the things I slowly, but steadily, changed in the way I parented my son during his schooling years:

- The mother–son personal bonding time was always during his school drop time. Though not daily, on the days I did drop him to school, we used to talk on the way and exchange stories, thoughts, and just about anything else.

- My contribution toward my son's academics was minimal because of the full-time job that catered to the financial needs of my family—my son and I. Thankfully, my mother took up the responsibility willingly and supported my son in his academics. I accepted that being a full-time mother who also had to work, it would be difficult to attend to every aspect of my kid's growth, especially the academics. So, I was more than happy to accept when the elders in the family offered to wear my hat for some time. This also helped me to avoid the role conflict that sometimes can be confusing for kids (between mother and tutor). They do tend to listen to others more than their mother, especially in a tutoring role.

- My overanxious parenting methods driven by the fear of "what the society would say," was suffocating my child's freedom of choice and expression. I never gave him the option to choose or decide for himself. It was like I was holding the kite close to my chest because I was afraid of it being ripped in the wind if I let loose the string tied to it. Little did I realize that my hold itself was damaging it more than the wind would. My child's behavior served as an alarm for me to take a step back and give him some space and freedom to explore, learn, and grow.

- I started to realize that my son imitates my behavior. I was made aware of this harsh reality when my son showed me the mirror by mentioning that he was just following my example, especially when he yelled and screamed during stressful (for him) situations. This is when I clearly realized that I was the one modeling the behavior that he was exhibiting. I understood that this meant that my insecurities would become his insecurities tomorrow and would have to work on them and reshape myself to be a better role model. This thought made me consciously change my behavior, both as an individual and as a parent.

- I encouraged the habit of book reading and insisted on him having physical activities outside and inside the home. The main driver for this was to reduce his time spent on gadgets. The secondary reason was that he would get a better understanding of the household chores and it would reduce his dependency on others for getting his personal jobs done. In the long run, it would make him self-sufficient, which would be an asset when he eventually had to move away from home for his higher education or work.

- I involved him in all household activities, be it housekeeping, cooking, cleaning, or whatever else it may be. I felt that it was important for him to understand the concept of load sharing and gender equality. I did not want him to fit into the normal gender patterns that are followed in many Indian households even today. The recent pandemic has taught us many things in life, this being one of them. Such actions will make him more self-reliant and appreciate the work others do in the family.

My son's behavioral changes and his approach to dealing with situations brought in me, as a parent, a complete transformation from the person that I used to be.

- I was someone who used to think academics was everything and used to get upset if my son's performance in tests and examinations did not meet my expectations. Now, I have realized that there is much more to life than just academic performance.

- Earlier I used to thrust my opinions and decisions on my child. I do not do that anymore. We have an adult-like conversation on our respective views and then finally I leave the decision to my son, who is now in his mid-teens. I have refrained from intruding into his personal space and let him mull over by himself before he decides on something.

- I am grateful for my parents being an integral part of my life and my son's. When I was in school, there used to be a period for

Moral Science. Now the school curriculum does not have this. I had my parents and brother, who spent a lot of time with my son, telling stories that had moral values and encouraged personal interactions with people rather than gadget dependencies. They would also play with him making the human interaction a lot more engaging so that his dependency on gadgets was minimal. I was willing to let go of my anxiety of wanting to always be that person who runs his life for him.

- I started treating him as an individual, respecting his voice, thoughts, and ideas by giving him a listening ear. We (me, my parents, and my brother) developed the habit of open communication with my son. At any point, if we differed from his point of view, we ensured that we did so without disrespecting or rejecting his point of view. We shared our suggestions on how he could do better for himself after we appreciated him for his current efforts in school or anywhere else.

***

The divorce proceedings began when my son was 2 years old. It was at this time that I completely lost hope in my marriage. I did not want the confusion about when the father of my child would enter our lives to add more emotional baggage to what we both were already carrying to the end.

The divorce turned into a long-drawn custody battle which ended only when my son was 11 years old. My son first faced his father when he was 9 years old, in court. This was mandated by law as it was the father's visitation rights. While my son knew he had a father who was not staying with us, I never spoke about my issues with my spouse till this moment when he had to be brought to court. The reason I had to share was to prepare him mentally and emotionally to meet his father face-to-face for the first time.

The discussion was not the easiest for me, and I am sure it was not easy for him to hear it from me. His silence for the next few days told me how difficult it must have been for the child that he was. The feeling of dread combined with anxiety is difficult to explain in words, but that is what I felt. My stomach felt like a bottomless pit when father and son met for the first time in their life. I was more concerned that my son did not get emotionally hurt by anything he heard or saw on the court premises. I was surprised at the maturity that my son showed in assimilating this information, the proceedings, and the in-person meeting with his father before facing the one question he had to respond to.

When the question was presented to him to choose which parent he wanted to be with, he chose me and rejected his father. Even when he met his father for the first time, he did not express joy or even curiosity. I saw caution and a lack of trust in the way he saw and spoke with his father.

Now my parenting journey is a lot more enjoyable and interesting. The first relief was the finalization of the divorce and child custody, which removed the anxiety of uncertainty of the father claiming rights over the son. In addition to my full-time job, I now have a business that is a year old. It is a boutique that caters to women with sarees, salwar materials, and handmade jewelry in stock. I enjoy the sourcing process for the saree and the salwar materials. Jewelry making is my passion and catharsis. This is when I meditate and unwind from the everyday stressors that I have accepted as inevitable.

My son is now at the age where I treat him as a friend, peer. He knows that I am always available for him at any time in his life. He is free to explore, stay curious, fail along the way, and learn and grow. As a child born in the digital world, he knows a lot more about it than I do. He helps me learn and understand the digital space while he also manages the social media handles of my business in a way that will appeal to the current-day digital customers of my boutique.

He is part of the grown-up conversations as well. In a year, he will be in college and then as an adult he will have to face this big-bad world on his own. While he knows that the family and his mother will always be there for him, we cannot be the ones making the decisions for him. So, by actively engaging him in discussions concerning the family's functioning, any business transactions and status, investment options, and any other life-related discussions, we make sure that he knows what it takes to run a household. The hope is that this will help him manage his life when he leaves the nest.

"Treat others the way you want to be treated" are the words that I keep reiterating to my son. These words may sound simple, but they have a deep message about empathy and compassion. The one sure way to teach him to be empathetic, caring, helping, and say sorry with genuineness whenever the situation demands, is to practice these in our lives. This is how we build character as well as strong relationships with others where we value the relationship over being "right" as dictated by society or our ego.

These changes in my parenting methods and my outlook helped me to parent a strong individual, who is now independent enough to make decisions related to his academics and extracurriculars. While he loves the elders in his life a lot, he does not depend on them for his life's decisions. There are times he advises and corrects me when there is a fork in the path ahead of us.

I have come a long way in my personal and parenting journey, and I cannot wait to see what my future holds for me as a parent to such a sorted and grounded young adult who is clear about the major things in life. I hope my parenting journey does help you find your grounding through some of the life lessons I learned along the way.

Chapter 9

SUPPORTING YOUR CHILD IF THEY COME OUT TO YOU

Anuradha Gupta

"Remember that your child coming out to you is an act of deep trust, so it's really important to let them know you love them just as they are."

—Aruna Rao

This chapter will take you about 20 minutes to read, give or take. In this time, according to the Trevor Project (a leading nonprofit which provides crisis intervention and suicide prevention services to LGBTQ+ under 25), in the US alone, 27 LGBTQ+ kids would have attempted suicide (one every 45 seconds). Tragically, this is the second leading cause of death in this demographic. And these kids are not statistics. Like any other kids, they are deserving of love, a sense of security, and happiness. And our support could be life-altering and lifesaving.

***

What is the LGBTQ+ community and what does "coming out" mean?

If your child comes out as LGBTQ+, you may wonder what that means, and I hope this helps.

The LGBTQ+ (also called LGBTQIA+) community stands for lesbian, gay, bisexual, transgender, queer (or questioning). The plus stands for other identities like nonbinary and pansexual. Queer was once a slur that has been reclaimed by some. They are also called the "gay" community, a term we will sometimes use in this chapter.

In the term LGBTQIA+, "I" stands for intersex, and "A" for asexual.

Together, these include sexual orientation (like being lesbian) and gender identity (like being transgender), with gender expression also discussed pertaining to how we express our gender, our clothes, hair, and so on.

Some parents are told that this is a new phenomenon! But you would be surprised to learn or may already know that the gay community has always existed with accounts from the beginning of recorded history, like the *"tritiya prakriti"* or "third gender" in India, the "golden orchid" society in China that encouraged lesbian relationships, and the "two-spirit" Native American people who embody both feminine and masculine energy, honored with many spiritual and social roles.

LGBTQ+ people are just who they are. Their identity cannot be altered. Just like I cannot turn Caucasian.

To "come out" is to reveal your identity or sexual orientation to someone. Why do people feel so alone or "different" when being LGBTQ+ is so natural, normal, a part of their identity, and common? I learned that one to two percent of people are intersex, meaning they could have reproductive tissues that do not fit in with the binary of male and female. Many may not even realize that, while others are subjected to non-consensual surgeries by their families when they are little. They often suffer from dejection and depression, feeling left out and alone. And that is one or two out of every hundred people ... a precious part of our society.

Let us say your sex assigned at birth is female. Have you felt guilty, torn, and absolutely beside yourself with fear about whether your family or the general community will accept you if you are attracted to a man? Have you ever had trepidation about having to go and tell anyone? About "coming out" as straight?

The gay community on the other hand is a marginalized minority that is still fighting to be accepted for who they are and for basic rights across the globe. All are based on the belief of heteronormativity and genders being binary. Nature does not have two genders. We "tolerate" attraction only between men and women, as if it is for us to police. This marginalizes the LGBTQ+ minority leading to ill-treatment and creating cruel legislation against them.

It is no wonder many people, even celebrities have "come out" as LGBTQ+ late in life, from Canadian actor Elliot Page who came out as transgender at the age of 33, to American stand-up comedian Wanda Sykes at the age of 43, to American broadcast journalist Anderson Cooper at age 45. Indian LGBTQ+ celebrities include filmmaker Apurva Asrani, author Vikram Seth, environmentalist and gay comedian Vasu Primlani, and trans actress, Bobby Darling.

Karan Johar, a popular director-producer in Bollywood has been very private about his sexual orientation and it is no wonder since it was only in 2018 that LGBTQ+ relationships were decriminalized in India. In his biography, *An Unsuitable Boy*, he wrote, "Everybody knows what my sexual orientation is. I don't need to scream it out. And if I need to spell it out, I won't only because I live in a country where I could be jailed for saying this."

If it is hard for a grown adult, you can imagine how hard this is for a child who is uncertain about how their own family will accept them, let alone what is in store in terms of the community or legislation.

***

What is the status of LGBTQ+ rights and how are they treated the world over?

Some of this may be daunting but I wanted to share the statistics with you, so your parent bear kicks in... bear with me! Knowing these facts and stats has helped me to grow my understanding of how best to support and advocate for my child.

LGBTQ+ folks are regularly subject to inequality and violence from society, and that is just one of the reasons that injustice should not begin at home. A cloud hangs over them as it is, what with unfriendly legislation, and having to counter bullying and microaggressions all by themselves.

When we think of LGBTQ+ rights, we often think of acceptance and dignity. Sadly, being LGBTQ+ is illegal in many countries (currently 69). This is particularly a legacy of British colonialism with anti- LGBTQ+ laws that persist in 36 out of 53 Commonwealth nations like Malaysia.

Gay rights vary across the world. Being gay is illegal in Iran, and in Saudi Arabia, you could get killed for being LGBTQ+. In the UAE and now possibly Uganda, there is a death penalty attached to being gay.

It was only in 2011 that the United Nations Human Rights Council passed a resolution on LGBTQ+ rights. Things have gotten better and like India, many countries such as Angola have decriminalized gay relationships, and same-sex marriage has become legal in many nations including Argentina, Australia, Germany, Mexico, and South Africa.

Same-sex marriage is legal in the US since 2015. Yet, depending on the state you live in, you may not have equal rights related to education, employment, healthcare, or housing. You may struggle with punitive state laws pertaining to everything from bathroom access to sports to gender-affirming care to book bans. More than 430 anti-LGBTQ+ bills have been introduced this year alone by April 2023—mostly impacting the mental health of gay kids, causing terrible harm to their sense of security, and restricting access to healthcare.

The gay community encounters 4x higher violence, and intolerance and homophobia only fuels this. Many states allow "conversion therapy" which tries to forcibly "convert" people using inhumane means and can lead to trauma, depression, and suicide.

In fact, only 21 out of 50 US states offer LGBTQ+ people lawful protection against discrimination. In schools in the US, around 8 out of 10 children report being harassed because of their gender identity or sexual orientation (according to the nonprofit, GLSEN).[1] LGBTQ+ kids risk abuse at home or being thrown out. Self-harm and suicide rates are high.

When it comes to how gay people are treated in the US, the statistics mainly from Trevor Project's latest survey are dismal.[2] Forty-five percent of LGBTQ+ youth seriously considered attempting suicide in the past year, 73 percent reported symptoms of anxiety, 58 percent reported symptoms of depression, 36 percent reported being physically threatened or harmed due to their gender identity or sexual orientation, and nearly one in three were homeless. Almost half of transgender people were sexually assaulted and intersectionality worsens these statistics.

What would propel a person to come out in such an environment? Some people say they are indoctrinated and some say that this is a lifestyle; how could it be? Knowing that things could be difficult, only one thing could make a person feel like they should come out—that they want to be authentically themselves. And another reason possibly could be that they trust you. It is a badge of honor to wear. They do trust you.

***

I would like to share two stories, two possibilities. Both are inspired by real-life stories with identities masked. The context and content have been altered.

Scenario I: (Content Warning: Suicide)

Bharti spent many years in the closet. She just did not see many people who were "out." And, no wonder, LGBTQ+ relationships were criminalized in India till 2018. She did not have any role models or ideas of how people could live their lives and be happy, successful, hold a job, thrive, and most importantly, be accepted by family and loved ones.

In college, over time, she could come out. It was like a weight had been lifted. When it was time to go back home, there she was, back in the closet. Her family joked and asked her whether she liked any guy. Or even dated someone.

When she started working, her parents told her it was time to look for a match. She first told her mother about her identity. That night, they turned her out. She went and stayed at a friend's house because she could not afford housing. She had to blend in, which meant risky behavior. Substance use and drinking were common. It was hard to keep a job. Over time, she became an addict. Tragically, she died by suicide. Her family was devastated but in time, her mother pushed through her pain and advocated for LGBTQ+ rights as best as she could and supported families like themselves.

Scenario II:

Bharti spent many years in the closet. She noticed that her family was open about LGBTQ+ identities and relationships. Someone talked about a gay movie that they did not denounce. Someone mentioned a gay celebrity and they took it in their stride.

She realized she was a lesbian at the age of ten and continued to feel that way. Finally, at the age of 16, she decided to come out to her mother. She got a hug and the assurance that she did not need to worry. Her father took some time but he too came around. Her mother realized how much discrimination Bharti was likely to face and her Mama Bear instinct kicked in. She built an army of aunties who went to Pride wearing the most colorful rainbow clothes.

Bharti literally had to tell her mother that there was more to her life than being a lesbian and set a limit on her enthusiastic support, but she loved it. Her family had her back. She thrived, went to BITS, Pilani, and found the GSA (Gender and Sexualities Aliiance) Club, Anchor! She recorded podcasts, wrote articles, and even met a girl she really liked. It was not all rosy, there was homophobia to contend with. It could get hard. But she could be herself and she thrived.

***

Why should you support your LGBTQ+ child? Or any LGBTQ+ person?

The statistics I mentioned are chilling. We are still imploring people to be inclusive because "someone you love" could be part of the community. Consider the following:

- Alan Turing, computer genius and code breaker during World War II helped end the war earlier for the Allies and saved countless lives. He was himself subjected to "conversion therapy" by the government and tragically, died by suicide.

- Many of us have heard of Florida's "Don't Say Gay" legislation. Talking about being gay is considered a "mature" topic. That is because people are looking through the lens of sex. When we tell a kindergartener that someone has a Mom and a Dad, they do not think of the sex they may be having; so, why should they do so when we tell them they have a Mom and a Mom? It is actually absurd to think so; we are surrounded by "straight" images of people kissing in Disney movies. People like Anita Bryant, an American singer known for her anti-gay views ran a campaign in 1977 to repeal a local ordinance in Miami-Dade County, Florida, that prohibited discrimination on the basis of sexual orientation. Gay people were accused of being pedophiles and groomers which is horrifying. And this anti-LGBTQ+ movement has started again in the US in full force to garner votes.

- There are hopeful incidents like the Stonewall Riots, a series of spontaneous protests by members of the gay community in response to a police raid back in 1969. In the words of Martha P Johnson, the Black trans icon who was arrested during the riots, "No Pride for one of us without liberation for all of us." In 1999, June was declared as Pride Month, a celebration of the LGBTQ+ community.

It can get discouraging but for every step back, there is a major step forward. And in this environment, here are the reasons to support your LGBTQ+ child:

1. **Survival (support is lifesaving):** We all want our kids to be happy and healthy. Every 45 seconds an LGBTQ+ kid attempts suicide. And even one affirming adult could reduce that probability by 40 percent. Be that adult. Save lives.

2. **Health challenges:** The LGBTQ+ community is faced with mental and physical health challenges, barriers to healthcare, and minority stress on account of how they are treated. This could very well be secondary trauma based on the homophobia they see around them in real life or in the media. Your support is healthcare.

3. **What will others say and why does that matter?** Many people are footballs of other people's opinions. They are worried about how people will treat their kids! And how will you treat them? If the neighbors are gossiping and that scares you, imagine how vulnerable your kid is feeling. You being

an anchor and teaching them resilience will truly count and inspire your kids, and others.

4. **An opportunity to grow:** Your child has given you a beautiful, unique opportunity to grow and learn. Embrace it! Here is a minority community that has, all at once, become yours. There is so much to advocate for. You are part of this journey; your children are not broken, they do not need fixing, but they do need your affirmation.

5. **Combating misinformation:** The earth has always been round, rotating around its axis and revolving around the sun! Yet, during the Dark Ages, such scientific utterances were met with great oppression. The LGBTQ+ community is still at that stage. Lies, propaganda, and misinformation abound. People go to any lengths to penalize gender outside the binary and relationships that are not "straight."

Here's an example. As part of anti-LGBTQ+, particularly anti-Trans propaganda, people say that gender-affirming surgeries are done on little kids without due process but that is misinformation. Also, medical institutions across the US have supported gender-affirming care as lifesaving.

6. **An end to systemic oppression:** Sometimes, it is easier to stand for social justice when it is not close to home and for some, it is the other way around. Either way, it is hard for us to see anyone ill-treated. Empathy and a desire for change takes over. It may be your child. It may be someone else's child who faces inequity and injustice. Every drop in the ocean, anything we do to make things better will be a step to end systemic oppression.

Here are some of the ways you can support your LGBTQ+ child when they come out:

1. **Love is a process**: Some of us profess unconditional love for our children. The act of being a parent is tough. You may feel hurt, angry, upset, and confused when your children come out and that is fine. You have to shield your child from even yourself as you process your feelings. Your child is not letting you down. Your kid is being incredibly brave and trying to be themselves. Return their trust with love as you go to the next and important step in this journey.

2. **Educating yourself**: Your child may have told you they are non-binary. Or they are lesbian. What does it mean? It is time to read up more and educate yourself about identities and honoring them, from gender expression to pronouns to chosen names. I went through a course, "Queering Identities" that touched upon their history and their struggle to live a dignified life. It was eye-opening and reaffirmed that LGBTQ+ folks have always been there.

3. **Seeking resources**: Your kid is going to need resources and you can be the bridge. You can find resources from books and organizations like PFLAG, GLSEN, HRC, and GLAAD in the US. In India, Sweekar is a good resource for parents and platforms like Gaysi Family, Sahaay, Queer Ink, etc. for the community. Through your own study, you can seek resources for your kids. If health resources related to say, gender-affirming care are needed, how do you find credible ones? If mental health resources are needed, what do you do? Find LGBTQ+ affirming healthcare. If they are exploring their identity or sexual orientation, find local resources like the Trevor Project in the US.

4. **Finding an affirming counselor**: Your child or you may need counseling. Do look for an LGBTQ+-affirming counselor; many therapists will state clearly that they support the

LGBTQ+ community. There are a few medical providers who may be homophobic, and it is good to do your homework.

5. **Finding peer-support groups like GSA clubs:** Locate peer-support groups in your district. A GSA Club, a Prism Club, and a support group for you as a parent may be a great start! There is nothing more comforting than finding peers on a similar journey with its ups and downs and trials and tribulations. You could also help educate others. I often talk to the larger community about Hindu gods that are LGBTQ+ or how existence is half Shiva, half Shakti and therefore non-binary.

6. **Movies, media, and celebrities:** Our home had a family *Schitt's Creek* evening every Saturday and our favorite movie was *Birdcage!* Other favorite movies like *Love, Simon* and *Badhaai Do* had us in splits! So many of our children's friends came out to us because they felt safe. Normalizing LGBTQ+ media really helps and celebrities do so much more. They demonstrate that gay folks can shine in all fields; arts, STEM, as writers and leaders, in politics, in the corporate world, and so on.

7. **Not outing your child without their permission:** It is wonderful to support your child but do not "out" them without their explicit permission; some situations and places can be unsafe or uncomfortable for them.

8. **Shielding your child from bullying and abuse:** It is a sad fact that compared to our LGBTQ+ children, we do have privilege. The prospect that they may face bigotry can fill us with anger, grief, and even a sense of helplessness. Depending on the situation, if they are being bullied, we can step in and report bullying or use whatever tool is appropriate.

9. **Tools to manage their mind:** The daily challenges get amplified for LGBTQ+ children. Teach them tools to manage

their mind. Meditation can help manage stress, anxiety, and trauma. Research has shown it can also help reduce implicit biases according to a study published in Psychology of Consciousness in 2016. Andrew Nunberg, PhD, Ayurvedic coach, LMT, and Art of Living meditation teacher, who lives in the US with his husband, has this to say: "Meditation does help us safely process all the stresses we pick up on a daily basis and that's where it's really key for marginalized communities. For a few minutes each day, we go to a place that is beyond identities. We simply exist and those moments are incredibly uplifting and healing."

10. **Joining LGBTQ+ organizations:** There are many LGBTQ+ organizations that tirelessly advocate for the community and educate the general population about their identities and the issues they face. Joining an organization as a volunteer would help you be part of your child's journey in a way that can help many more families and empower you.

11. **Keeping abreast with developments:** I was very moved by a plaque that a parent carried at Pride, "I want my children to know I didn't remain silent." Over time, anti-LGBTQ+ legislation goes back and forth and stresses our kids out, impacting their mental and physical health. It is a good idea to keep track of these developments and speak up where you can.

12. **For emergency management:** If your child needs support, or you or any LGBTQ+ youth you know is in crisis, reach out to the Trevor Project 24/7 at 866.488.7386 or thetrevorproject. org in the US. You can also call the 988 Suicide & Crisis Lifeline at 988, text HOME to the Crisis Text Line at 741 741, call 911, or go to the nearest hospital emergency room. In India or any other country, call local helplines or go to the nearest emergency room.

***

When you hold your newborn in your hands for the first time, your heart is filled with love and tenderness. You want nothing to come in their way, no shadows, no pain. You wish them all the joy and blessings. You want to believe in them, you want to elevate them, you want them to thrive, and you want to pass on none of your trauma or sadness ever.

You learn that what matters most is being good enough. Doing good enough. You want to just try your best. You will make mistakes and you will go back and say sorry and that's part of parenting and being a good role model for them to have, knowing that no one is perfect. Part of trying is loving them fiercely and unconditionally. If your child comes out, if you feel like you have feelings to process, do that. If you feel like you need to learn, then learn.

The LGBTQ+ community walks in our midst. They are our family. They are our friends. They could even be our own children. And so many are in the closet scared to be themselves. They do need to know their existence is precious. If your LGBTQ+ child comes out to you, do embrace them and support them with all your heart, because the world often gives them the opposite signal. How can we stand by and let that happen to our kids?

NOTES

1. "The 2019 National School Climate Survey: The Experiences of Lesbian, Gay, Bisexual, Transgender, and Queer Youth in Our Nation's Schools," https://www.glsen.org/research/2019-national-school-climate-survey
2. "2023 National Survey on LGBTQ Youth Mental Health," The Trevor Project, https://www.thetrevorproject.org/survey-2022/

Chapter 10

RAISING CHILDREN IN A VIRTUAL WORLD

Jaita Mullick

"The highest education is that which does not merely give us information but makes our life in harmony with all existence."

—Rabindranath Tagore

Under the expanse of the enticing blue sky, with the soft, dreamy clouds drifting away, I swing to and fro with the breeze lifting my hair, as I dream in the green acres of cornstalk. Another time, I lie under the bed with a Nancy Drew in hand, transported to a land of mystery and adventure. Sometimes I chase my younger brother till I catch up with him, and we both dance and giggle in the magical rain pouring from the rumbling sky. At other times I sit beside my grandfather or aunt and listen to tales from afar of days gone by painting those pictures in my mind with the brush of palpable imagination.

How do we bring this magic into the lives of our children growing up in a virtual world?

The virtual world that we live in is superimposing, all-encompassing, and almost magnetic! Sometimes, I look back at those hazy days, where time stood still enough for me to breathe in the beauty of my surroundings, experience the enchantment of a childhood novel, and enjoy quality time with my family across generations, and I wonder what might be missing for my child growing up in such a fast-paced, always online, digital age? As American filmmaker Ira Sachs once said: "There's a lot of things lost in the Digital Age." How can we tap into the brilliance that our digital world provides without losing the beauty our natural world has to offer?

It seems like the rise in digitalization has brought with it an all-so-common parenting struggle in whether to befriend our children by allowing them to watch their favorite show or be strict for maintaining the TV-watching rules of screen time that we set for them. As can often be the case with parenting, sometimes it feels like you can never win!

In this chapter, I wish to share with you the journey I have been on to discover a healthy balance for my family and share lessons learned along the way, offering my tips that you can use and experiment with.

***

There's no doubt that the world we live in today is vastly different to that of my childhood. I have grown up through the most rapid period of digital expansion to date. Technologies which seem second nature to my child were unimaginable to me at the same age. It is fair to say that I am an analogue parent raising a digital child!

Digital technologies have profoundly changed what it means to be a child today. How children learn, connect, relax, and engage with the wider society is often influenced by the internet and accessed via devices, smartphones, social media, and messaging apps. The rise of the information age has brought with it many benefits: school life continued remotely throughout the global pandemic (albeit with definite challenges and inequalities); digital devices offer more inclusive learning opportunities; and there is ample opportunity to connect with and grow from interactions with peers from across the globe.

However, along with the clear opportunities the digital age brings comes a diverse range of potential risks and harms that we as parents are so acutely aware of. As many of these technologies are quite new to us too, the numerous unknowns can create understandable cause for concern on how to make the best choices when raising children in a virtual world. How do we educate our children on the use of devices safely and resourcefully? What digital training and upskilling do we, as parents, need to keep up to speed? What is the latest research and advice on the "right" amount of screen time for our children to protect their physical and mental wellbeing and growth (The World Health Organization recommends no screen time for babies under 2 and no more than one hour of screen time a day for those aged 2 to 4.[1])? How do we help them to navigate the pressures of social media, stand up to cyberbullying, and protect them from any form of online harassment and abuse?

There is a lot still to be discovered by both parents and children alike on how best to, purposefully and safely, navigate today's virtual world. With the internet and related devices now being such an integral part of our everyday lives, I see myself on this journey with my daughter as both the teacher and the pupil.

***

It was the fall of 2019. My little one was 2 years and 5 months old. We went on a trip to Europe. We faced our share of challenges in trying to manage a toddler and planning the trip keeping her age in mind. At times we would be so exhausted that we would just give up and hand over the mobile phone to her! But that is not the end of the story. Even the phone would not do the magic! She would only want to be with me and would not go to her father or be in the pram. We realized it was a new country with very different weather conditions and my child was finding it hard to adjust to it. But the crux of the matter is that the all-encompassing virtual world failed to soothe her. And the fact is no gadget or digital technology can replace human connection!

Another time, we went shopping at the local mall. I and my daughter, Adriya went toward the sofa in the waiting space and occupied a corner while my brother was trying on a few shirts. In the room, waiting, were a lady, a little girl, and a man. All three were staring at their phone. I realized my daughter would also feel the urge to watch something on the phone. To avoid that, I stood up and walked toward the huge mirror and started playing "Reflection, reflection," a game that I created in the spur of the moment. Adriya found it interesting, and she too showed her palm once, then her knee, and her hand and we giggled and had fun!

I have always been a conscious parent since the time my child was about a few months old. On her first birthday month, I had gifted her, her first flip and flap book. While nursing her, I used to make facial expressions and tell her stories. As she grew up, her love for books and stories increased, but there is no denying that along with it also increased her curiosity for the screen! I too as a parent find it difficult to limit my daughter from excessive use of TV or mobile phones at time, but I have been able to limit the usage of the screens or her interest in these digital gadgets.

During our childhood days, we had simple games to play: role-plays, outdoor games, and indoor games like puzzles, chess, ludo, and so on which kept our mind agile and body active. Mental and physical dexterity go hand in hand. While growing up I never felt the pressure of studies which cause so much anxiety in today's generation of kids. Outdoor activities kept the mind sharp. Instead of counselors to ease the stress, I had my gang of cousins with whom I engaged in activities such as sky-gazing, mindless laughter, or mimicry of each other and so on. It is these fond memories that help me find different ways of engaging with and entertaining my daughter in today's digital age.

***

Screens, in any form, are catapulting and satisfying to the mind. Such is the hold that we may be ready to forgo everything else to experience this instant pleasure and sense of achievement. The 24-hours live cartoon channels or video games provide an easy solution to boredom. But I have chosen to steer away from such default solutions. On more than one occasion I have experienced cold stares from the people around for not budging from trying to raise my daughter in a digital world with limited access to the digital media, but the mother in me did not slacken. Stories, books, songs, and baby talk always came to my rescue. Once, while we were having dinner at a restaurant, I noticed how a mother had to resort to the mobile phone to persuade her toddler to eat. My alternative approach has been to bring along a story book, and ingraining the habit of book reading from an early age has supported its success. Blocking out the feeling of staring eyes when you choose not to select the instant solution of the device can be challenging; external pressure is everywhere in parenting! But staying focused on the parent you want to be and how you wish to connect with your child is more important.

For the children of the alpha generation, boredom comes easy. With a short attention span and everything within their reach requiring no effort to negligible effort, thanks to the advancement in technology, this generation loves speed and instant solutions to everything. For instance, while going on a trip, they want the tablet as they get bored during travel. Similarly, while waiting for their favorite food item to arrive at the restaurant, they need the phone to avoid boredom. Nowadays even the sight of the playground does not allure some of them.

Let us move ahead and see if getting bored is really a bad thing. What does "I am getting bored" imply? It simply means the child has time in hand and does not know what to do with it. Is it really bad to get bored? Not at all! In fact, when children have free time in hand, we, as parents, need to divert their attention to constructive thought processes. For instance, while traveling in a car, if your toddler is finding it difficult to channel her energy, you can suggest to watch the scenery outside by pointing out specific things or actions so that she can draw them later or both of you can discuss how the scenery changes. Look how we are moving but it seems the fields, trees, and huts are moving even faster! I keep a story book, a slate and chalk, and a drawing book with color pens always in the car. When my daughter has already watched the scenery and people outside, these things come in handy. Alternatively, you can play *antakshari*, that is, songs we sing by taking turns, or backward number counting, or making sounds of different animals by turn.

As parents, we need to help our little ones realize the value of free time or leisure time. This is the time to think and be creative, try new games, draw a new design, or role-play with the doll. Did we have so many games, gadgets, or friends while we were growing up? We knew how to draw happiness and excitement from gazing at the stars, from watching the birds fly, from feeding the ants, from playing hide and seek, from taking Mumma's saree or scarf and fashioning into our dress while spotting a red *bindi* on the forehead, holding grains of puffed rice between the lips while pretending to be a ghost and scaring the elders away, and, of course, how can we forget the "bor-bou khela" where I would become the bride (bou), my brother the groom (bor), and a cousin would be the priest or priestess getting us married, and that would be so much fun! Innocent and simple games but they remain etched in our memory! Let us bring "boredom" back so that we can guide our little ones in the path of nature and nurture with simple and basic joys of life. If you reflect back, you may re-discover many such instances from your own childhood too. Try using such games or activities to help your child find a healthy balance within the virtual world.

Nowadays children have an action-packed day monitored closely by their parents. We generally follow a daily routine in raising our children so that we can teach them the value of time. For instance, wake up at 7 a.m., followed by catch the school bus at 8 a.m., then return home at 3 p.m., do homework till 4 p.m., have evening snacks and go out to play at 5 p.m., music class at 7 p.m., and so on. Why not twice a week or so keep a time duration for doing nothing! Yes, I mean doing absolutely nothing! And do it consciously so that as much as children know how to follow a routine, they should also know how to value the free time at their disposal, undictated, and untrained.

A few months back my toddler picked up the word "boring" from her friends and then whenever she did not have a playmate, she would utter "I am boring" implying "I feel bored!" While going somewhere by car, I heard her say this again! I tried explaining to her how "boring" is good. It gives us time to think and create new games or try our hands at playing something we have not done for some time. But that was not enough! Now comes the turning point and how... After a week or so we went for our planned trip to my hometown Kolkata. There the lifestyle is very different. She did not have a nanny to take care of her nor the usual friends or a specific school, play or study time. She has her aunts and grandmoms who would play with her during their free time. But the rest of the time, she did something new, she learned something new, and that was the fun and adventure of exploring a new place and meeting new people! She would roam around the entire house discovering "secret doors" and meandering paths through the maze of staircases, one room leading to a bigger room or new people who told her tales about the abandoned house nearby or why the cat comes calling daily at 2 p.m.! She was so much in awe and mesmerized with everything that she forgot the word "bored." She started creating new games, for example, with chairs stacked against one another to create a stage. We became her audience, she a rockstar singer! Not that she did not know this, but routine life had somehow eaten away the fun and thrill of exploring the unknown! The best part is we were back from our vacation, and she somehow forgot about getting bored!

We as conscious parents sometimes try to cram every bit of the day with useful activities. But what we do not realize is that children do not see the value and hence they will not take such effort with gratitude. Instead, they express a sense of dejection and helplessness. On the contrary, let them really feel the urge and learn more about the activity that they want to take up, be it playing guitar, learning to dance, playing badminton, and so on. When you feel they are keen and are ready to take up the challenge of learning it, gift it to them and they will be grateful to you for trying to understand them, their needs, desires, and aspirations.

***

I and my husband try to be communicative with our daughter. In helping your children find a healthy balance with screens, nothing works as effectively as open communication. A few days back my child came up to me saying "Mumma, what is disgusting? I heard it in so-and-so cartoon." Instead of telling her it is a bad word and outrightly ordering her to not use it, I tried explaining it to her. "When we don't like something, we term it as disgusting. But our planet is so beautiful. So, can anything be very, very bad? And if something is bad, we have to find out why it is bad and make it good. But if we label it as disgusting it will never become good again and this goes for persons, places, or things. Is there something which you find disgusting? Let's both try to find out why it is so bad." She understood and did not use the term again. But there will be times when the generation will have their own lingo and you will need to create a bridge to secure the gap.

Children as young as 3 years want to be understood like adults, and these days we as parents try to give them that respect by being clear, specific, kind, and compassionate in our words. Try to explain to your child the ill-effects of prolonged exposure to the digital media. Simply telling them a "no" means "no" is not enough. Befriending them is a better way to make them listen to us. This works with my daughter. If I or my husband explain to her the reason behind why I am asking her to do or not do something, she values our openness with her and tries to follow what we say.

And then they will also have to face peer pressure from a tender age. I try to limit screen time to an hour every day during vacations and to weekends during school weeks. But then wherever she goes outside, she sees children with mobile phones and then realizes that I limit her phone usage. To avoid the repercussions, I let her play around or I play with her through some simple verbal games or let her get engrossed in reading, drawing, etc., even when we are outside our house for a family dinner or while going on trips. I try to involve her in discussions so that she does not feel left out. In spite of this, there have been trying times such as when we were returning home from a Pondicherry trip, and the traffic jam on the highway was unbearable. We were almost 2 hours delayed.

That is one instance when all the regular activities that I reserve for Adriya when she is traveling by car were exhausted, and it was a one of a kind of situation. Sometimes in such situations I let her watch a cartoon episode on the phone, but I always try to explain to her and help her understand why it is best not to use phones for an extended span of time. Whatever may come, do not make it a subject of your ego. When you shout, "I told you not to do this and you are not listening to me at all! You have become a brat!", you are damaging her more. Be flexible according to the situation. You are the parent, and you are the best person to decide your actions according to the situation.

***

For holistic child growth and development, we need to be personally invested. In the words of Keith Krueger—CEO of the Consortium for School Networking (CoSN), a nonprofit organization that serves as the voice of K-12 school system technology leaders in North America—"It is important to remember that educational software, like textbooks, is only one tool in the learning process. Neither can be a substitute for well-trained teachers, leadership, and parental involvement."

It is easier said than done. With some of us managing parenting single-handedly, or having two or three children to raise simultaneously, or simply looking for some quality time with our partner, it is not always easy. At times, we may resort to virtual devices and that is absolutely fine. In this fast-paced world we need to slow down at times and relax.

Throughout the day, whatever activities the child does are all related and make them who they are. Here are some of the suggested steps and best practices to ensure the positive involvement of children with the virtual world that I have come across and experimented with on my parenting journey so far.

Encourage empathy.

According to Diya Chatterjee, a clinical psychologist, currently working on Problematic Internet Use (PIU) in the Indian youth, "Staying hooked to virtual platforms can reduce a child's ability to pay attention to tasks offline and their ability to empathize with peers which would get expressed as long-term deficits in interpersonal relationship building skills."

Empathy is an essential human quality which is the base for a successful personal and professional life ahead. When the world is going through a crisis of all sorts, the need of the hour is empathy. And we can start to encourage empathy in our children through very small activities away from the virtual world: asking the child to help us with household tasks such as folding clothes, washing utensils, tidying the house, arranging flowers in the vase, letting them take the lead in choosing vegetables while doing grocery shopping, and so on.

We can introduce our children to social service. Take them along with you to care homes and let them spend time with the residents; hearing their stories and sharing theirs. Let them realize the joy of giving. On weekend mornings, introduce them to pet gatherings in the parks if such activities happen where you live.

We all lead busy lives and the comfort of having some time on hand when our child is watching content on the mobile phone appears precious. But it is necessary to monitor the content and draw the boundary of a time duration. There is a lot of variation in the quality of content available to them! For instance, you can converse with your child about what appears on the screen or laugh with them while they are watching or initiate a conversation after the session. Be with your child for the first 10 minutes and later you can let them watch on their own. Encourage them to help you choose the time limit for device usage, for example shall we say 15 minutes to 30 minutes of TV today, setting the boundary together.

Most importantly, introduce them to their extended family. Video calls cannot replace the fun of meeting relatives and cousins and spending time with them. Though video calls are necessary these days to conquer the distance between families, and we feel a sense of comfort in being able to see them, for child growth it is essential to let them meet their family members at least once a year if that is feasible. Children find it hard to relate to emotions through the virtual space. For my child I really had to coax her to say even "hello" at times over video calls and then I started visiting my hometown once a year. That is when I saw a marked change. She would remember the people she met with specific memories and would easily ask for them on video calls. The virtual world is immensely helpful but without empathy, it is futile, and we, as parents, have a huge role to play in supporting its development. In trying to balance work and life we need to ensure we are still role modeling empathy for our children.

Enhance attention spans.

For young minds to develop, it is essential for them to be able to concentrate and focus. While listening to stories, their ability to concentrate develops. They visualize the entire scene through their world of imagination. I try to read out stories to my little one on a daily basis. And this has been our daily routine since she was 3 months. I have used all sorts of books—musical books, touch and feel books, and pop-up books. And now at 5 years of age I do see a visible impact.

I do not refute the fact that this daily practice takes time and patience, from first you telling the story in baby language, then in your vernacular, then gradually telling in English in your own words, progressing to narrating the story in the words of the book and finally she starts reading herself. It is definitely painstaking, as some days you will not have the urge to emote and use a variety of tones and sounds while telling the story. But, trust me, it helps immensely! I have found my daughter to be hooked to books like nothing else. Not that she will not watch TV or will not be attracted to mobile phones but the love for books is equally, if not more, enticing for her! She does not mind putting in the effort to read every line of the book and pays attention to what is being narrated. She is curious to read stories filled with suspense, mystery, adventure, or fun! And that is my antidote to her screen time attraction! You might find something else that works for your child. It could be music that helps them to focus and concentrate.

Nowadays children as young as 12 years have their own mobile phones or voice-activated assistants. We as busy parents feel a lot at ease when we know the whereabouts of our child. But we definitely need to be careful about the use of such gadgets by young children as this is the time for molding the young minds.

Children today have a lot of amenities at their disposal, and they may not always realize the value of things. We cannot blame them for this. We are living in a generation which believes in use and throw. Analyze your child to understand what kind of toys appeal to them—motor, sensory, visual—and draw them towards these.

According to Neha Jain,[2] a passionate owner and founder of The Kahaani Box, a library for children:

"Reading can help reduce screen time for children as it is an alternative activity to watching TV or playing video games. Reading requires concentration and focus, which helps children to develop longer attention spans. This can help reduce their desire to constantly switch between screens and activities.

When children engage in reading, they are actively using their brains and imagination, and are less likely to seek out the passive stimulation that screens provide.

Reading can also be a more fulfilling and rewarding activity for children, providing them with a sense of accomplishment and helping to build important language and cognitive skills. By encouraging children to read, parents can help them establish healthy habits and reduce their reliance on screens.

When screen time is reduced, children also are protected from Blue Light Exposure from screens which in turn helps promote better sleep hygiene.

The internet can be a great source of information and entertainment for children, but it can also expose them to inappropriate content that can have negative effects on their development. Unfiltered videos during screen time may lead to cyberbullying and other forms of online harassment which may negatively a child's mind.

Overall, reading can be a healthy and beneficial activity for children that helps them stay away from screens and develop important skills and habits."

Monitor screen usage before bedtime.

Do you have a TV installed in your bedroom? When the TV is in the bedroom, it provides the potential for unlimited access to content without any proper schedule. The widespread use of portable electronic devices in the bedroom leads to insufficient sleep. The blue light from the screen is very disturbing for sleep patterns to establish.

If you co-sleep with your child, ensure their access to mobile phones or TV is restricted much before their bedtime. Do not encourage screen time before bedtime by being mindful of your own behaviors. Instead, replace evening screen time with activities such as reading, coloring, family conversations, and so on. Try to jointly develop sleep routines if possible as we, the parents, also need to disengage from the use of screens in the evening to improve our quality of rest. We need to set examples for the youngsters to follow. Because when we use our phones late at night and then ask children to stay away from them, it is expected that they will rebel. They do not see the justification and simply ordering or shouting at them will worsen the situation.

I have a work shift that requires me to attend meetings and be on my laptop till late into the night. I always explain to my daughter the reason I am not able to sleep with her and that I would sleep later. Sometimes I read a story to her if I know I will not be able to sleep with her at the same time. Sometimes my husband will put her to bed.

Set a few house rules.

If your child is used to following house rules from an early age, they will respect the limitations. For instance, I have decided a specific time when my child can watch cartoons. Using the phone is not essential for them at all. So, you can show them an educational program on the mobile phone on a Sunday for half an hour or so. Also, monitor your phone usage in front of them, especially mindless rambling on social media which we all indulge in to kill time! Ensure that you are not using the phone throughout the day watching videos, reels, and movies in front of them. Remember children will think, "If you can do this, why can't I?" Setting the right example is important. Mealtime for my daughter is always without the TV or phone. We as a family try to have meals together during the weekends.

Parenting is teamwork. Needless to say, always include your spouse or other family members in your child development plans. Each child is unique and has different needs. Customize your strategies according to the disposition and interests of your child.

Ensure you and your child have a lot of fun and exchange of ideas in the process!

Slowly reduce engagement time with the virtual world.

We cannot avoid the screen when schools ask children to watch certain videos on YouTube as homework assignments or do research on the internet for project work. And of course, there are benefits to be gained from using quality digital resources in a focused and meaningful way. But we can look to reduce engagement time with the virtual world where it serves less of a purpose.

Study carefully what interests your little one has. Try introducing them to different genres of music, listen along with them, and tell them interesting facts about music. You can get a pet for them. Do some daily activities like planting, dancing, or playing games. Take them to a children's library and create genuine interest by discussing the books with them. You can try "no-fire cooking" with them. Let them prepare a simple breakfast for the family and you can cook his or her favorite item for lunch as an incentive. Take them for star gazing and short morning treks.

Try to engage your child in playing outside and engage yourself in the playtime sometimes if not daily. The more they are engaged in various sports such as swimming, playing football or basketball, or simply playing in the sand, the more it helps in reducing time spent in front of the virtual screen. I try to engage my child in painting pots, pebbles, or bottles to decorate the house with and let her do random things like playing with water toys.

Human interaction, both inter- and intra-personal, is necessary for healthy development. No matter the digital advances of this age, human–technology relationships need to be closely monitored and kept within healthy limits to ensure that the advantages do not get over-ridden by their potential disadvantages. Every child is different, and as parents we are best placed to set the digital boundaries that work for our families. Let's bring all the wonderful sources of magic, found beyond the virtual world, into the lives of our children.

NOTES

1. World Health Organization, "To grow up healthy, children need to sit less and play more," April 24, 2019, https://www.who.int/news/item/24-04-2019-to-grow-up-healthy-children-need-to-sit-less-and-play-more
2. Personal communication with Neha Jain, the founder of The Kahaani Box.

Chapter 11

GIVING YOUR BABY A VOICE AND A CHOICE

Arren Williams

"When it is obvious that the goals cannot be reached, don't adjust the goals, adjust the action steps."

—Confucius

I have been graced with this wonderful opportunity. Presenting a topic on modern parenting to a worldwide network of parents is both an honor and a bit of a challenge. As parents, we have a wealth of personal experience. As humans, we are individualistic and dynamic. Although we are from the same planet, we have evolved into unique groups with separate cultural centers, religions, philosophies, languages, histories, and child-raising styles. No matter how different humans seem to be, we also have many similarities. Most of us do share a common desire to express ourselves. Not only do we want to communicate, but in many cases throughout our history, our lives depended on our ancestors' ability to do just that. We are thinkers and talkers. Through clear, intentional conversation, shared thoughts and concepts can develop into solutions and greater understanding. Language is a fundamental building block for all societies and civilizations.

What if babies could do this, converse? When asked what subject has had the greatest impact on me personally, as a parent, as a grandparent, and as a childcare provider; what topic would be of global interest, utilized, and beneficial... My subject, most definitely, is baby communication. Not the goo-goos but actual conversations with our babies.

New parents today can be overwhelmed, sleep-deprived, and left wondering why their baby did not come with a manual. So, what do they do? The responsible thing, of course, is research. They look for tools to help their babies and themselves. With the addition of the internet to our daily lives, we have been flooded with a plethora of great information, diverse information, mediocre information, and misinformation. New parents can easily become perplexed by the sheer volume of protocols and programs that tout they are the answer and the way!

One thing that I know for sure, there is no one way! I have witnessed the clearing away of stacks of "how to" baby books, the deletion of baby protocols and programs, and the discarding of non-functional archaic beliefs that do not apply anymore. Progressive parents are instead implementing a more intuitive, personal, and collective approach to child-rearing. Parents and childcare providers are combining ancestral ways with modern practices, protocols, and products. They are picking and choosing from the familiar, and the foreign, to best serve the child and the family's needs. This brilliant new way of doing things has shown greater flexibility and a deeper capacity to see each child as an individual, and as an individual that is part of a complex social structure, our families.

While infants and babies are learning our languages, they struggle. What happens when babies are sad, in pain, hungry, wet, tired, or angry? They cry, sometimes throwing their entire bodies into their plight. Their lack of verbal skills is a frustrating obstacle to obtaining their solutions. Parents share in this temporary language barrier. New parents can often reel from the meaning of tears, cries, the sources of a malady or discomfort. Any confusion and uncertainty felt by the parent, or care provider, is then non-verbally and/or verbally communicated back to the baby, creating more frustration and a cycle.

This cycle deserves a closer look. With our lack of understanding, we combine our inability to speak the same language, as we are attempting to communicate complex concepts to babies who do not yet understand. Everyone is frustrated, and then we do it all again, in tones that are musical with nonsensical words that are not real, but rhyme. I believe there is a better way to talk with our babies.

Babies thrive when they are addressed with care, and spoken to in an appropriate tone, using real words. This form of *clear communication* can be our first step in developing conversations with our little ones. When we are suffering, nothing replaces snugs and hugs, yet understanding the whats and the whys of a situation helps us to connect the dots and communicate on deeper levels. It is similar for infants and babies. Their minds are constantly at work developing a better understanding of this new world and their place in it. They are continually growing and striving to include us and to be included. As parents and care providers, we can close the communication gap by giving our babies an early voice.

***

How do we give babies a voice? This was the question that I pondered over and over. Years ago, one of the infants under my care had the most awful ongoing bum rash. It broke my heart to change her diaper while she was in such agony. I comforted her. I distracted her. I was intentional, efficient, and empathetic. What we needed though was a bridge to understanding, a pathway to reasoning.

After evaluating our agreements and our oppositions, I realized that both my baby and I had clear intentions and needs. She was in pain and did not care for any more pain. After many diaper changes, she and I both understood that changing her diaper was going to inflict more pain. I had a need for her to understand that I was there to be of service and care for her, not hurt her. I needed to explain to her that the rash would get worse if not cleaned properly and that I was so sorry for her distress. Communication was our goal and our obstacle, and we were not moving forward. It was time to adjust our goal or to adjust our action steps. It was my experience with this lovely baby that created a need in me to find a way to use clear communication to establish early understanding.

Verbal communication is a learned skill. With a few tools and repetition, babies can associate and connect words with concepts, people, and things. Clear communication is the opposite of baby talk. It is the intentional and repetitive use of common small words, in a calm and appropriate tone, to form a communication base. Through this use of a repetitive dialog of vocabulary words, babies find their voice. This practice quickly opens up a dialogue. Once babies can express their needs and wants, they can also start to make choices, and then collaborate. I have always used *clear communication* with my children, grandchildren, and my clients' children. Speaking to babies using real words, with clear intent, encourages them to contemplate cause and effect, presenting the options that come from choice.

The concept of *baby choice*, of baby empowerment, is a modern idea in the West. As a mother in the 80s, I was what others considered controversial. Many of my unique approaches and techniques of child-rearing were frowned upon then yet have become commonplace and practical today. Fresh whole-food feeding of infants has replaced jars and prolonged formula use. Baby and child yoga are becoming a part of daily home routines. Baby, and child, full-feeling expression is an encouraged and normal practice today. Baby talk is being replaced with *clear communication*. Allowing my children to have a voice and a choice were particularly unacceptable concepts then, yet now are being seen as beneficial tools for baby and child development.

The philosophy of *baby voice* and *baby choice* translates into free will. By giving babies a voice that will evolve into a choice, many stumbling blocks, especially those associated with self-accountability, can be easily navigated. By allowing babies to experience and explore their choices, in a controlled environment, they learn quickly with little to no blame displacement. Their choice, their outcome.

When our little ones are born, we look upon their little hands, their precious tiny toes, so small, and vow to love them, protect them, and let nothing ever happen to them. We have been entrusted with nurturing and growing this amazing being and we are on the job! They are so helpless, so vulnerable, we vow to lift cars off them if need be! Admirable, yet none of us are superheroes, not even on our best days.

As parents, we provide, protect, prevent, love and teach. Even so, our babies are going to experience some challenges as they navigate this big new world. We cannot prevent all of life's bumps and bruises. We can utilize life experiences as tools to help not only our babies grow, but all of us grow. By adding early language, through *clear communication*, we can enrich our babies' early experiences and help them learn to expedite their own solutions through learned skills. This increased understanding elevates our babies' ability to reason and make positive choices as they grow into children.

The concept of prevention and protection, like most things, is applied differently by different parents for different children within their family cores. One child in the family may be accident-prone while another is stable on their feet and rarely loses their balance. Individuality makes it difficult to construct a universal approach when focused on the concept of protection, prevention, and baby pain. What if we re-work these concepts? What if we look at our babies' small ouches as points of prevention, and also as tools for comparison, compassion, growth, and understanding?

Modern parents are not sitting back and resting on the laurels of the parents that came before them. They are testing, experimenting, and doing what feels right for themselves, their families, and their babies. Parents are teaching their babies that they are individuals with value. To increase their understanding, their ability to communicate, and their recognition of potential sources of bumps and bruises as they grow, some modern parents are asking their babies to choose (within moderation), and to be accountable for their choice, and its outcome.

***

Going back to my baby girl with the diaper rash, I can now see how I could have done things differently. I could have broadened both of our perspectives by using words that defined her condition and expanded her perception while changing her diaper.

Words like YOU/YOUR, OUCH, CAREFUL, GENTLE, OKAY, CHOOSE, SORRY, BETTER, and HELP, are great to utilize when helping a baby understand and process the pain of a bum rash. These are complex words that present advanced concepts. Once these words are a part of the baby's internal vocabulary, they are available for many other teachable moments. Nothing motivates us more than pain. Brains become hyper-focused and retain the information surrounding pain and its source. Although rashes are common, they are painful. When addressed, and cleaned with empathy, and compassion, they can also serve as a beneficial part of the learning process.

Knowledge obtained through a painful experience is sticky. We tend to remember these lessons clearly with a depth of detail including smells and tastes. Pain, for a baby, is just as memorable. The vocabulary words that you choose to use while addressing a baby's painful needs can have a lifetime of results, good or bad. Babies are looking to you to guide them. They don't understand yet. A clear indicator that your baby is in pain is usually expressed by the baby through tears or anger. There are also some physical indicators that can clue us into their plight.

While undoing their diaper, if there is a noticeable drawing up of the infant's legs, a slamming down of their feet, a guarding of their privates, or excessive wiggling and turning away, they are usually attempting to communicate with you. These actions can be indicators of pain, and a clue that moving forward with intention, and focus, is recommended. These are moments of deep empathy and compassion. We hate to see our babies and children in pain. This type of pain can be terrible and is hard for the infant to process. "Why are the people that care for me hurting me?" They have no concept of what must be done to prevent further rashes and more pain! All that they know is that their loved ones are hurting them and that makes their pain your fault!

Crying and anger displacement are natural responses to pain. No one likes pain. Most of us avoid pain at all costs. So, what do we do? Do the change faster? Do the change as fast as possible, creating as little discomfort as possible? Put them in a warm bath and gently clean the affected area? I am sure that we all have applied these techniques and others, depending on the situation and our physical location at the time. How about using this moment to do what does not feel natural for most parents and care providers? What if we slow down and use *clear communication* to expand the baby's perspective, understanding, and vocabulary?

Once pain is identified the following conversations may sound like this:

OH NO! OUCH! (Identification of pain.)

SO SORRY that YOU HAVE AN OUCH! (Empathy, possession, recognition.)

I WILL HELP YOU! (Support, solution, teamwork, identification of possession.)

OKAY? (Asking for permission.)

I MUST CLEAN YOUR OUCH (Affirmation of needed procedure, teamwork.) OR YOUR OUCH WILL GET MORE OUCHY! (Possession, defining cause and effect.)

I AM SO SORRY THAT YOU HAVE AN OUCH! YOUR OUCH is so OUCHY! (Reaffirming possession, empathy recognition.)

I WILL BE GENTLE! (Reassurance, empathy, intention.)

OKAY? (Asking for permission.)

I WILL BE CAREFUL. (Personal accountability of diaper changer, assurance, recognition.)

GENTLE, GENTLE, GENTLE. (Reassurance of the level of care.)

OKAY? (Asking permission.)

While this may appear to be unnecessarily complicated, or a way too in-depth analysis of the simple action of a pre-diaper change, I assure you that it is not. We have set the stage for great growth for both parties. While preparing to clean the affected area you are implementing *choice* as a variable, establishing a team concept, and initiating the use of *clear communication*. You have identified possession of pain, and as a result, prevented blame displacement and you have opened up a dialog that they are active participants in. We are asking for their understanding and approval, we are confirming our understanding and intentions. Of course, if they said no, the diaper would still need to be changed. Yet, it has been my experience that, even though the baby knows from experience that there will be discomfort or pain, 99% of the time my baby will grant me permission. Acceptance of my help may be communicated by relaxing their legs, unclenching their fists, and un-scrunching their faces. The tears and anger will stop, and they will become relaxed and compliant.

So now for the diaper change, right? Not quite yet! Now the use of segues and distractions can be included to deepen the baby's state of relaxation and provide a connection through the discomfort. Songs and stories, the introduction of a favorite Lovy or stuffed animal, and a pacifier combined with things that the infant can hold onto, work well to occupy their minds through the discomfort. I will offer several things, YOU CHOOSE! (Choice); blowing bubbles on their bellies to make them laugh, or counting toes, or shadow images from your hands on the wall by their heads, or whatever works for the baby.

Once they are relaxed, then it is time to remind them of what needs to be done before starting:

SORRY, WE MUST CLEAN YOUR OUCH NOW, OKAY! OKAY? (Empathy, confirmation of needed procedure, possession, recognition, asking for approval.)

While cleaning the area, the use of soothing words and empathy may sound like this:

I WILL HELP YOUR OUCH GET BETTER. (Personal accountability of the changer, aid, teamwork, possession, promise of improvement.)

GENTLE, GENTLE, CAREFUL. (Reassurance of care.)

When the affected area is clean, it is beneficial to let the area air out. By blowing on the inflamed area, or fanning it with a new diaper, the baby is immediately distracted from the previous pain and is soothed. This also expedites the healing of the rash and moves the mindset of both the baby and diaper changer onto a more relaxed state.

This may sound like this:

ALL DONE! (Completion.)
WE HELPED! YOUR OUCH WILL GET BETTER NOW! (Teamwork, aid, possession, recognition, promise of improvement.)

Depending on the client, salves or ointments may be required. Before closing up the diaper, an explanation of the application of salve, or ointment may sound like this:

I WILL PUT THIS ON. (Showing them the salve, intention.)
IT WILL HELP YOUR OUCH GET BETTER! OKAY? (Defining benefits, aid, possession, promise of improvement, asking permission.)

This practice of *clear communication*, with empathy, and compassion, not only soothes and educates the baby, but it also helps both the baby and changer through a rough spot. Through repetition, this practice will instill a trust bond between the baby and the changer of mutual respect and understanding.

Wow, right? All that in one diaper change? Through the use of the words, YOU or YOUR, we have established ownership of the OUCH, the pain, eliminating blame displacement. We are a team solving their problem, together. Through word associations, and using *clear communication*, we are broadening baby's vocabulary by introducing words that are vital for future teaching moments. Later, at about 4- to 7-months-old, these words can help the baby self-assess and problem-solve. When posed with questions that possess words that the baby understands, the baby can communicate a desired solution by gesturing. When a baby is allowed to express their big feelings, they can do so without placing blame.

Remember, infants are looking for solutions and bridges to better communicate with you, just as badly as you are! Questions and statements like Why are YOU crying? Do YOU have an OUCH? Are YOU HUNGRY? Are YOU SLEEPY? Be GENTLE! How can I HELP? Is that OKAY? YOU CHOOSE? Are you SORRY? are now understood by the baby, and they can also be answered by the baby as well. By posing questions with familiar words, babies will find an answer for their current dilemma, and then communicate it back. By giving babies a voice, and a choice, they will assess, problem-solve, and propose a desired outcome.

Babies know our excitement, and frustrations, our pain, and our joys. They KNOW! They are master manipulators and survivalists! Infants are powerful beings who will grow and learn with, or without, parental input. As adults do, babies all learn differently and are stimulated by different things. Being an active and passive observer of their growth, we can empower them to grow independently, and still be an active part of their team.

I ask my babies to self-assess. I empower them to problem-solve through personal *choice*. I explain why what happened, happened. I encourage their use of their *voice* and opinions. Unless they are SLEEPY or HUNGRY, and then all logic goes out the window. We all know what that looks like, don't we?! So, to recap, through the consistent and repetitive use of empowering words, and *clear communication*, you can initiate *voice* and *choice* as concepts, with clarity and comprehension, empowering your baby, and instilling an understanding of accountability.

Wow, right! I bet you are already doing most of this and did not even realize the significance and ramifications! This is next-level stuff! As the baby develops and starts to roll over, the words that you choose to teach, through repetition since birth, are already a part of their internal vocabulary. Statements like BE CAREFUL. THAT WILL OUCH! PLEASE NO PINCHING, GENTLE, GENTLE! SORRY! IS THAT OKAY? are completely understood. Now the other words start coming into play.

The big-feeling words like KIND, MAD, HAPPY, SAD, and EXCITED ... are fun to teach and become quick *clear communication* tools. When an infant hands you a toy, THANK YOU THAT IS KIND OF YOU, as you hand it back, HERE, FOR YOU! THAT IS KIND OF ME! Handing it back is very important because they really never intended for you to keep it! It is practice for them in environmental manipulation.

Big-feeling words allow baby to express their BIG FEELINGS. We all need to express our BIG FEELINGS and know that this is definitely a learned skill. Encouraging babies to express themselves is important. Anger is the trickiest of the big feelings. The direction of anger at others should be quickly redirected. The concept is simple; it is okay to feel angry, it is okay to express anger, and it is not okay to direct anger at others. Big-feeling words empower infants, babies, and children with the ability to understand their BIG FEELINGS, associate possession of them, and communicate them back. This expands their understanding of choice, the accountability for those choices, and the concept that we all make our own choices, even parents.

***

The concepts of *voice* and *choice*, along with empowerment and accountability, are the keys to self-growth and understanding, and they get stronger as the child grows. Babies that are given the space and freedom to grow, explore, and express themselves, fail and improve, with passive and hands-on interaction, grow into confident humans. This not only prevents the re-working of unproductive, non-serving habits and mindsets, but it also alleviates the trauma associated with these tendencies and beliefs and the recovery time needed to correct them. Deep-seated trauma takes much work to overcome. Life has its share of trauma already. It may be best to prevent what is logical and to prepare our children for what we cannot prevent.

Since this chapter is based on babies, they have been the primary topic discussed so far. Let us touch on our other precious family members, our children, and our parents. As a childcare professional, many of my clients have multiple children at various stages of development. As we grow as parents, we find that what works for one child does not for their siblings. We also as parents are evolving and growing every day. We realize that our new skills were not around when we were raising our older children. This dynamic state of growth and application can create rifts sometimes, and pose challenges as we work together to create harmony in our homes. I am sometimes hired to assist families to assess, propose, and implement strategies to help them meet their desired goals of change in patterns and habits.

Once habits are formed, they take a consorted amount of effort, and much repetition, to change, or redirect from these patterns. They are quite sticky. We all know this as adults. How many times have you asked yourself for change? What does it take to make that change? Why not prevent these undesirable habits from birth, or correct them as young as possible? Babies have a clean slate and can be directed away from undesirable habits. As we grow older, we need to look at the source to correct these habits.

"Where's my shoes? Where's my ...?" These common questions are clues that the older kiddo that's come under my care may lack a sense of self-empowerment and accountability. Work in this area may need to be done. I first observe then I assist families to change the habits and patterns of older children. I become a detective and sleuth out the clues by asking questions. How strong are the empowerment skills of the parent? Are they like I was, doing too much for their children? Does the child self-motivate? Problem-solve? Does the child realize that they are the one choosing? Does the child realize that their lives belong to only them regardless of their situation? Do they tend to act or react? Do they understand that *no one is the boss of them, but them*? What is the source of the immediate need for the child to seek out someone else to solve their issues for them? Is this from trauma or past failures? Is this from a child's sense of entitlement? Of inadequacy? Are their actions based on the accelerated performance of an older sibling? These are some of the queries that I pose to myself and analyze. Once we, as a team, have determined the source(s) we can then work on a solution of empowerment and accountability that fits.

This is what I do. I take my clients to the next step toward their specific goals using logic, and mutual respect, but mostly kindness. Nothing works every time in every way. No child, infant, or person is the same every moment of every day. Internal and external forces are always at work. We are not always present, or our best selves. This is all a part of the human condition. Parents are no exception to human frailty.

As parents we are sometimes overworked, sleep-deprived, "hangry," stressed, uninterested, overwhelmed, distracted… The first step in addressing any issue, or situation, is to look deeply at ourselves. This may seem very bizarre and foreign. Many of the behavioral issues that I have witnessed in children are generational patterns that were created by the parents, and by their parents before them. The "Mom, mom…MOMMMM!!" behavior, is a common pattern that I have found in family units where the parents are overwhelmed and therefore distracted. These parents have way too many things happening at once and cannot focus on, or validate the importance of, the child or children's voice, or needs. Therefore, the child acts out. This becomes a pattern for the child of feeling unimportant, resulting in insecurities. They will seek validation from others, and they are sometimes not choosy. With focus, intention, and help, these patterns are redirected, course-corrected, and harmony reinstated. Through small habit changes and focus, parents can empower themselves to be accountable to their needs first, plan for success, then communicate clearly, and give the child, children, back their *voice* and *choice*.

Families that work through these, and many other types of difficulties can move on to the next level. These next-level families are powerful units with a set of powerful individuals. How did they become that way? Some started with their first child. Most of my families are works in progress, just like mine. They are evolving, learning what works, applying those concepts as tools, and growing some more. They are finding self-awareness and growth, through personal voice, choice, and accountability. They then apply this knowledge, and growth, to the family dynamics as an individual that is part of a team. These are all learned skills. Through patience, kindness, integrity, mutual respect, and repetition, we are all capable of the growth that we choose.

***

Choice is the *choice*. Humans grow exponentially with the implementation of free will or choice. How did I get to this truth? To understand why I feel the way I do, it is important to see where I come from, and my family's history. The philosophy of free will, of choice, was a foreign concept for most women growing up in the '60s. Women were raised to be wives and mothers governed by the men of their families. Abandoned by my father, my brothers and

I were raised by my grandparents, while our uneducated mother scooped ice-cream to support us. My 70-year-old grandmother was the matriarch of our family. She was taught, and therefore believed, that children were to be seen and not heard. I had no voice, and was not permitted the expression of any feelings, or desires. I knew that this could not be the way. I vowed to do it differently, to parent with purpose! To give my children freedom, and a *voice*!

When I had my daughter, I swore that she would have her own *voice*, and the opportunity to be whoever she wanted! I gave her complete freedom just to be. However, with no tools and no mutual respect, we floundered. I reverted to my childhood education of service to others and not to myself. By my selflessness, I taught her to not truly value me, because I had no value for myself. She could not be a part of a team, because I was not on anyone's team, I was cheering from the sidelines and hauling water and snacks.

By my second child, I focused on trying to fix these deficits. Unfortunately, I was not successful. My son was kind and loving, but I was still doing all the work. This prevented him from having a clear sense of self, from taking risks or asserting himself and growing to his full potential. As a result, he developed a habit of blaming others for what should have clearly been his responsibility. So, yes to free, to kind and to loving, and no to self-empowerment, self-accountability, and we still had no team concept. I had not figured it out yet.

By my third child, I had it all figured out! Love, self-respect, teamwork, self-empowerment, and accountability would prevail! Nope! My third child was very sick from birth! Hospitalizations were common, frequent, and ongoing through her teens. Instead of implementing my well-contrived plan, I fell into a pattern of overcompensation for all my kids. For my older two, I plied them with activities and gifts, because now most of my free time and energy was spent on keeping their baby sister breathing. To make up for her hardships, I spoiled my youngest with stuff and things! By this time, I was also a full-time working single parent, juggling way too many plates.

What was missing in all these scenarios was teamwork and my own sense of worth as a parent and a person. I had to retrain myself, to teach my children, that I had self-importance and a voice, and that they have accountability and self-empowerment. As my family grew together, they also grew independently.

Today we share healthy, happy relationships full of mutual respect, trust, and love. We are a team of hard-working, hard-playing individuals that are kind and loving, with loads of big feelings! We are problem-solvers that reach far beyond our core family to aid our communities and the environment. This process has taken many years to correct many different issues. Many years of self-evaluation, self-permission, self-empowerment, self-authenticity, and gradual change for all of us. My grandchildren are now 10, 9, and 8. They are loving kind individuals that are self-motivated problem-solvers, and team players, who sometimes still cannot find their shoes! We obviously still have some growth to do!

***

Life is a work in progress. We each face new challenges and obstacles daily. Practice creates habits, that create life patterns, that open new life paths. As individuals, we must find what works. As families, we must work together to create patterns and rules that form tools. These tools, once applied regularly, and consistently, will provide a protocol, or regiment, that works for each of our families, a set of checks and balances. These tools are different for each family and for each person. It all depends on what the issues are that each person faces, and how best to serve the family as we make these desired changes. We need processes and tools to build us up and prevent us from sitting in the same circular holding patterns of dysfunction. I have given examples of *baby voice*, and *baby choice*, as tools to awaken in our babies a sense of self-empowerment and accountability. Yet there are many more tools out there. These are the ones that have worked for me and my clients. Choose the ones that work for you, and your family. Tools rule! Get them! Use them!

This is the best time to be human that I have ever seen. This is the era of the individual. We are melding and evolving quickly beyond gender and race. There are parts of our planet that are ahead and parts of our planet that are behind in this trend, yet as a whole, humans are becoming more humane. Through the use of *clear communication*, we can use our voices to express our choices with kindness and accountability. These are the gifts that I give to my grandkids. These are the gifts that I ply in my trade as a childcare professional with the over 100 children who call me Miss Arren. These are the gifts that I give myself!

Chapter 12

EMBRACING THE FUNDAMENTALS OF PARENTHOOD

Ramakrishnan Rajamani

*"When everything around us may seem to challenge who we are,
we need to know how to find certainty within ourselves about
what we want and what we believe."*

—Sue Knight

On the one hand, the world has become very small. One minute we are talking to a friend far away from India, the next moment we are watching a soccer match happening in Dubai on an OTT channel. We connect with friends across the world through social media chats, while talking to someone sitting next to us on the same couch.

On the other hand, with so much content to watch and information to consume, the great benefits of digital connection create the potential risk that we expect too much of ourselves and our children. We end up holding ourselves to perceived external expectations of what the world now demands of us. Our children too, set their expectations very high with many more opportunities for comparison.

This information overload can lead us, as parents, and our children to feel overwhelmed. As parents, when we are caught up in the distractions and high demands of today, are we missing our children's real need for human-to-human support?

I believe this is important regardless of the age of the children because we as parents are their true role models. Children learn from seeing, hearing, and feeling what their parents do! The first few formative years make a deep impact. In Tamil, my native language, it is said: "The flexing has to happen by the age of 5, or it would not happen even in the 50s." It is believed children feel their mother from the womb, learning happens from that stage, and certainly, they get to feel the emotions that the mother holds—be it happiness, sadness, or anger.

This chapter gives you a view of my learning and understanding of being a role model and going to the fundamentals for anything, and particularly parenting.

***

Whatever stage we are at in our parenting journey, there is an opportunity to set an example, by truly doing what we say and prioritising what is important to us in life. Let me share a story that I read a long time back, which has stayed with me when I think about what it means to be a role model. Once a mother took her child to Mohandas Karamchand Gandhi and complained that her kid was eating a lot of sugar. Gandhi asked her to come back after 2 weeks with her child. She went back to Gandhi after 2 weeks and complained about the same; *nothing has changed*. Gandhi said, *it has changed, I now have stopped eating sugar for the past 2 weeks, and now can talk about it to your son.* He could only make life better for this mother and son by first stepping back to truly understand the boy's perspective.

It takes a lot to do anything important, and certainly, it takes a lot to be a parent and bring up children! It is overwhelming and exhausting at each stage of child development. However, based on my experience and learning, I enjoy the journey with my son. This has been supported by going to the fundamentals, learning the structures, and applying them within this special parenting context.

Being a life and executive coach, I have learned not just from my life experience but also from others. This was made possible by learning neuro-linguistic programming (NLP). To me NLP is fundamental; it helped me to understand myself and other people at multiple levels—behavior, capability, beliefs/values, identity, and purpose. That understanding has helped me recognize patterns in myself and others and supported me to achieve desired results for myself and the clients I work with. I have since used the core principles of NLP in my parenting—replicating thought, behavior patterns and structure to produce excellence—to help me be a role model to my child. I hope to bring to life these experiences throughout this chapter.

The source of my NLP learning is the master trainers, Ramesh Prasad and Sue Knight. Ramesh is the founder of Onefluencer NLP Training and lives in Chennai. Sue Knight pioneered the use of NLP for people in business through her books *NLP at Work* and *NLP and Leadership*.

I have always believed in going to the fundamentals to understand and solve any problem; it helps me get a deeper understanding of truth. The metaphor for fundamentals I associate with is a plant in my garden. The fundamental requirements for it to grow well are fertile soil, water, and sunlight, and all of this in the right quantity.

Let me share a real-life story that touched my heart on going to fundamentals. A child was feeling sleepy in class and the teacher of the first session punished him by making him stand for the entire session. However, the second session teacher understood why he was sleepy and asked him to take a nap at the back bench for 30 minutes, and that gave him the energy and focus for the rest of the day. If that fundamental had not been taken care of, the child could not have concentrated for the rest of the classes.

***

This awareness took me to research the fundamental needs of humans. I found Maslow's "hierarchy of needs" resonated with me as it is simple and explains the basic needs of what motivates human behavior, based on five fundamentals: physiological needs (food, clothing, shelter), security and safety (health, financial, safety against injuries), love and belonging (friends, relatives, society), esteem (appreciation and respect), and self-actualization (self-awareness, self-development, reaching the potential). As a parent, beyond all of these needs, it is the desire that my child is *gravitated to living, kind, affectionate, true, focused, curious, creative, resilient, explores and enjoys life in his own way!* However, in today's world of distraction and high demand, this desire for living and simple enjoyment of life can get lost, with both adults and children at risk of moving away from focus areas or ambitions and what genuinely matters most to them.

I have sought to understand my child's fundamental needs at each stage of life, and I have learned some important parenting lessons along the way. The hierarchy of needs has to be nurtured in the right way, with the right significance based on the need of the child at every stage, and every child is different. This was a very big discovery for us as parents, as we made a mistake in the early formative years of our son. We were working parents and left our child with a nanny. While the nanny took care of our child very well, it was on the basis of her broad knowledge of nurturing a child. She took care of food, sleep, and safety; we were sure our child was in safe hands. However, neither she nor we had the knowledge or recognized the importance of the other, more specific, physical strength and social needs that he required until he reached the age of 5. Our son was overfed and overslept, and never asked or cried for food. We realized late that this was not helping him in the long run.

If we had this awareness about the importance of other needs sooner, we could have encouraged activities to enable and firm up his physique, such as going on a stroll, playing in the sand, enabling movement by play. We also learned that continuous talking to a child was necessary from the baby stage, especially given that we were a nuclear family and living in different locations (away from our hometown) in India, where multiple languages were spoken. Being working parents, and both of us minimalist conversationalists, our interaction with our baby was limited and it delayed his communication.

***

At the early baby stage, food, shelter, clothing, safety, love, and belonging (social needs) are of utmost importance. Babies are fed, made to sleep, given massages for healthy physical formation, and are also taken around in the sunlight, not just for nutrition, but also, so they get to see people and interact from that age by smiling, laughing, and crying in their own way. As a baby, their world is their parents, and they are particularly attached to the mother. At this stage, the mother's focus on her child is so deep, that it is beyond all distractions. For example, she can hear the child's cry from far off in the home, even if there is a loud noise from outside and inside the home. The mother has her eyes, ears, and feelings completely attached to the baby, as though she is still holding the baby safe in her womb. The mother nurtures by feeding, bathing, and protecting the child.

As the baby grows to the age of 5 to 10 years, fundamentals like food, shelter, clothing, safety, and social needs remain crucial. They start to connect well with other children, and it is very important for them to interact and move a lot physically. Observe a child sharing their experience of food and the importance that is given to it by talking about their friends' lunch boxes. They become expressive about their likes and dislikes as to their wants. In my experience, at this point, the child needs a safe environment to run around and play with his/her peers. They need to play a lot; playing in the sand is essential as it helps strengthen the fingers and legs. In our case, we moved our home to live within a community offering a lot of space and children to play with. We focused on nurturing our son in an environment that allowed him to focus, as distractions at this age are what they see, hear, and feel. We removed distractions from his study table and avoided conversations or TV during his study and skill-learning times.

Keep it minimal, let children get bored, and creativity starts! I learned this from my son's school, as the teachers had advised us to give him only three colors for his painting. It was tough initially for him in the early days, but later he was creative and started mixing colors to produce new colors out of it. This added to the value of minimalism and being creative. "Me love" being minimalist on materials, by nature I am a role model to my son. I keep required things on my worktable, and I make sure to clear the clutter after my work. It helps me to easily organize, be focused, and save time to do important things.

Children do not need to have a lot of things that overwhelm them; they do not need a cupboard full of toys that are not used. Even one toy that is used for days adds to the child's memory and it helps the child to do different things with just one thing. Early in our parenting journey we used to have a lot of things and he used to get distracted and meddle with things while learning. Now, we adopt various methods for his learning. My wife and I *support* my son by helping him clean up his table and keep the minimum required. He used to get a lot of toys as gifts, we moved most of the toys to the loft and gave him a few toys to play with at a point in time.

At this age children's self-esteem starts to develop. They want to be appreciated for small things that are done by them, and that encourages them to try different things and help build self-confidence and be interdependent! My son likes to paint and chooses colors that are not true to nature. Allowing him to paint things in the way he likes, and appreciating his creativity, has supported him to do more of it. When he was 7 or 8, he was painting scenery and painted a white crow. I was baffled, so I Googled and found there is a white crow and appreciated his creativity. He was happy. The outcome was he continued with his painting, sometimes it is realistic and sometimes imaginary.

It is this stage where emotional development also steps up; they understand the parent's emotions and moods (happy, sad, or angry), and so it is important how as parents we respond to events. It is said, give respect and take respect; at this age, they are like para puppets, they speak what you speak and behave how you behave. We would like our children to learn basic discipline and basic activities that we wish them to do! At this stage, they learn by seeing, hearing, and sensing, and the nurturing of these children happens by supporting them, telling stories, being a role model, and sometimes allowing them to experience a hard way by getting hurt and it is ok!

One of the key aspects I follow is one learning at a time, keeping one theme for a month or a few months, and using all learning methods for them to improve in that single area. This habit has also helped us bring our child up for the long term and focus on the outcome! We had a lot of distractions from the external world, but being focused on one fundamental has helped us and him.

***

As the children grow to the age of 10 to 15 years, it is another beautiful journey to just observe and paddle to navigate. For sure their fundamental needs like food, shelter, sleep, and safety are taken care of, which they by themselves are now aware of. With this awareness, the importance now shifts to social and self-esteem for them, which as parents we need to nurture. The nurturing now changes from doing and supporting *to* observing and supporting in a way they are ready to learn.

Continuing with the example of nurturing minimalism, as we expect it to develop creativity and resilience, we approached different learning models with our son. While we still supported him in cleaning his desk, we made him *experience* how focused completion of work enables quicker results, giving back more time to do other things that he likes. I *talk* to him while driving to school about various things, thoughts such as the wastage of natural resources in making things that are not used. I and my wife *share*, in his presence, things we do to stay minimal and how it has helped us in our development. As we watch TV (moral stories, mythology, documentary, children's channels) or read books, we *highlight* people living minimally and the value that they bring. I also invite my son to share his perspective on the choices I make, which helps my son to *think* and share his perspective and what he likes to do in that scenario.

The tough part of being a minimalist is the comparison with others. It is important that children understand that different people have different perspectives, and there are people in the world who are extremely rich and poor. At the end of the day, it is his choice, and he needs to go through his learning in his own way! Performing these role modeling activities, conversations, and scenario discussions has helped him get a better perspective on the choice he would like to take. He understands good and bad or right and wrong, and he takes the decision that makes him happy! Children are naughty, and we should allow them to enjoy being naughty.

***

As we step to the next stage of 15 to 20 years of age, children are completely aware of themselves, and much more physically aware. They are starting to understand who they are, and also have clarity on their wants. They are keen on their personal growth and are willing to work with their potential. However, they still need support for food, shelter, clothing, love, and bonding. As an adolescent, they start to take independent decisions on their needs and wants. They do not want to be told, as they know the difference between being right or wrong. Yet, they are prone to often be influenced at this stage by peer pressure.

Peer pressure could be direct or indirect. Direct peer pressure is based on people around them in the same socioeconomic circle, doing good or bad things. Indirect peer pressure is when they get distracted to become x or y or z because of indirect peer competition experienced through the world of the internet, without knowing what they truly want. Before the rise in digitalization, influence through direct peer competition was most common. Nowadays social networking groups which portray only the half-truth of individuals—and that is what the individual chooses to display to boost their self-esteem and be appreciated and validated by the world for what they have got—bring greater indirect peer pressure, which can be overwhelming.

I am not saying the world of the internet is bad. I just think it is like a double-edged sword; we need to learn to balance it and constantly review its advantages and disadvantages—where it could distract us from the fundamentals. The key is you being a model to help your children use the resource in the right way! Use the world of the internet for what you really want from it, and not for what it wants from you, and reach out to it when you need it! One way I manage this is by using a well-being app on my mobile to get the facts of usage and slowly cut down my timing on unwanted things! I have built a pattern in my day-to-day life on using social media, so my friends and family know I take time to respond, and if it is critically urgent, they reach out to me by a call. However, when I want information, say about a skill or the purpose behind some culture or the history behind someplace, I liberally reach out to the internet to learn from it.

In the company of their peers, with the world of information in their hands, children do not have to depend on their parents or the people around them to make decisions. The nurturing by parents has to be in a different format; children at this stage do not need any telling, yelling, stories, morale, or purpose (if you ask a teenager, they'll tell you that they already know it all and they expect respect for their knowledge). They just need a friend, a friend who can lend a shoulder to share happiness or to vent out their feelings when they are sad. A friend who equally shares his/her vulnerability and accepts the point of view and a friend who listens to their vulnerability without judging and being ready to support any time.

I experience being like a friend to my nephew; he reaches out to me when he is confused or angry, and he is comfortable enough to just give me a ring and talk to me, even though we live miles apart. For any suggestions or advice, he mostly has an answer, as he has gone through a lot of facts on the internet and spoken to other friends, but all he needs is a pair of ears to listen, which helps him think clearly as he speaks and make his own decision. Here again, NLP helps me to ask what it terms 'clean questions', that enable him to step forward and think even more clearly. This is what I do with teenagers through coaching to help bring them back to focus on important things in life!

***

Let me narrate an incident, from when my son was 8. On the way back from the office, I had picked him up and was coming home. I was a bit frustrated that day, and I spoke to him about something that happened in the office that I did not like and made the story simple for him to understand. He asked me to just enjoy the ride home and relax. By my actions, I had expressed my vulnerability, and in his response I could feel that he was already role modeling me in not fretting about things that were out of our control. By choosing to be vulnerable, we provide them with the key learning "no one is perfect." We also open the doors to our children to safely express their vulnerability, which helps them to move forward without the pressure to always excel and build resilience to face challenges by themselves.

Here is another example of me sharing my vulnerability to my son. I used to be nervous when talking in big town halls or when meeting with leaders. This nervousness sometimes resulted in my performance failure. After practicing the Swish technique, which breaks limiting behavior, and understanding my thought patterns through NLP, I overcame the fear of talking in a huge crowd. I shared this with my son and just like that I was his hero. In the case of this example, I was also able to demonstrate that failures can become steppingstones to success. In the longer term, this would be a critical learning for him.

We do make mistakes and it is all right! If you had personally misbehaved and if it was not the right thing to do, it is correct to say sorry and accept you could have handled it differently. Help teach children it is all right to make mistakes, so long as we learn from them! Everyone is human and is at different levels of understanding and emotional well-being at different points in time. We learn to understand the good or bad, and based on that we make a decision to move forward. This learning is fundamental for children too; they have to have the ability to choose the good or bad, and balance life to make sure life goes on, in the way they want it to. As a parent, being observant, and being ready to accept them with lots of respect and value for their decision, when they are stepping in to talk about it, is really critical. Being observant is fundamental to everything, you should observe their behavior and the tonality which represents their emotions.

From my experience as a coach to teenagers, I believe not many children like to be told what to do, and some adults too. They prefer to learn by experience or explore and role model someone's excellence! Sometimes others' excellence may not be appropriate for us. Once we realize that another's excellence or behavior is not our own and does not belong to our self-values or belief system, or culture, we can then decide to change the course of our behavior so that it connects truly to our beliefs and value system. Children often take the wrong path because of peer pressure and consequently lose track of their focus, but by being observant you can help them to identify this. Making the right intervention at the right time can help them realize their true potential and help them to focus and align to their values and beliefs through your coaching.

***

Parenting never stops! At the age of 40+ and as a child of my parents aged 80+, I still talk to my father as a friend about my vulnerabilities. He does not solve my problem, but my ability to move forward is the change he brings in! He does this not just for me, but for my siblings and my friends. At my father's age and with the experience he holds, he role models impressive levels of self-actualization. Probably that is why he just smiles at my problem points, to say that this too shall pass. He focuses on the fundamentals of living—love and relationships. My mother still shows her love by way of cooking food that I like!

***

In this chapter, I have used the word nurturing very often to iterate we do not build or construct our children. They are not robots to listen to what we say and act in a way we want them to do. I am sure we do not want a child who just does what is said without applying his/her mind. By optimally nurturing, we support them in a way, just like watering the plant with the necessary amount of water required at the right time, and we fertilize the plant at the right moment with the required quantity. We certainly do not flood or over-fertilize; we are aware of the right time and quantity by observing the plant turning yellow or touching the soil. And we do not kill the plant by not watering them at all. Everything needs a balance! At the same time, it is said, we should create some scarcity of water for the plant, so it understands the importance of need and strengthens itself during tough conditions. And this applies to nurturing your child!

Balance is key to every aspect of life. Help to enable children to understand the reason behind the differences in decisions based on environment and situations, and the child can always choose to decide on how he/she wants to respond when faced with the same. Nature balances itself in its own ways, mostly by self-developing and changing the atmosphere despite being overwhelmed at times with tsunamis, and erosions.

Parenting is a lot of work. It could be overwhelming along with daily chores, career, social life, and the need for financial stability; now, that could be a lot of distractions in day-to-day life. However, being mindful is important, take one thing at a time, one step forward on that one thing, and work toward it in a way you can use all the resources (people, capability, or things) to manage your life effectively.

By all this, you are being a role model to your child to focus on what is important to them at any given time. Use the resources in hand in the right way at the right time and take one step forward with an action that will create positive momentum. Take time to learn and grow from your experiences. Explore and enjoy this wonderful life journey.

To conclude, I believe the universal truth is that, if a seed is sown it has life; all it needs is a little nurturing over time. Clearly, it is the responsibility of all the adults in a child's life to support and encourage them. The question we need to ask ourselves is: how do our children experience the way in which we are interacting with the distracting and demanding world around us?

With these learnings, I invite you to my experience of the most fundamental thing of just being with your children in their development stages. Being available for them, by observing their behaviors, and helping to translate their emotions. Being available to them as a friend for them to reach out, by listening and nurturing with your learnings and experience, just point them to a direction for them to look up to for resources and answers.

And the most fundamental to all this is to shower abundance of *true love* on your children!

READING LIST

Aisling Leonard-Curtin and Trish Leonard-Curtin, *The Power of Small: How to Make Tiny But Powerful Changes When Everything Feels Too Much*, Dublin: Hachette Books Ireland, 2019.

Becky Kennedy, *Good Inside: A Practical Guide To Becoming The Parent You Want To Be*, London: Thorsons, 2022.

Benjamin Spock, *The Common Sense Book of Baby and Child Care*, New York: Duell, Soane and Pierce, 1957.

Carol S. Dweck, *Mindset: Changing the Way you Think to Fulfil Your Potential*, London: Robinson, 2017.

Geraldine Walsh, *Unraveling Motherhood: Understanding Your Experience Through Self-Reflection, Self-Care & Authenticity*, New York: Hatherleigh Press, 2023.

Richard Carlson and Joseph V. Bailey, *Slowing Down to the Speed of Life: How to Create a More Peaceful, Simpler Life from the Inside Out*, New York: HarperOne, 2008.

Spencer Smith and Stephen C. Hayes, *Get Out of Your Mind and into Your Life: The New Acceptance and Commitment Therapy*, Oakland, CA: New Harbinger, 2005.

Sue Knight, *NLP and Leadership: An A4 manual for trainers, managers and coaches*, Harlow: Peter Honey Publications, 2000.

Sue Knight, *NLP at Work: Neuro Linguistic Programming*, London: Nicholas Brealey Publishing, 2020.

Vicki Broadbent, *Mumboss: The Honest Mum's Guide to Surviving and Thriving at Work and at Home*, London: Piatkus, 2018.

Vicki Broadbent, *The Working Mom: Your Guide to Surviving and Thriving at Work and at Home*, London: Piatkus, 2020.

FURTHER RESOURCES

UNITED KINGDOM

Single Parents

Gingerbread is a UK-based charity campaigning for equal opportunities for single-parent families, who also offer information and advice to support single parents. https://www.gingerbread.org.uk/

Gender Diversity

Mermaids is a UK-based charity helping gender-diverse kids, young people, and their families, with a helpline service, training, and local support groups. https://mermaidsuk.org.uk/

Working Parents

Working Families is the UK's national charity for working parents and carers. They provide free legal advice to parents and carers on their rights at work. https://workingfamilies.org.uk/

Pregnant then Screwed is a UK-based charity dedicated to ending the motherhood penalty, supporting tens of thousands of women each year, and successfully campaigning for change. https://pregnantthenscrewed.com/

Founded by the lead co-author of this book, Jayne Ruff, Parenting Point helps parents find their meaningful and fulfilling work-life balance through practical, psychology-based workshops and coaching. https://parenting-point.com/

Special Needs Children

KIDS is a UK charity for disabled children, young people, and their families. They offer practical, life-changing, and creative support, empowering disabled children and young people to amplify their voices and champion their rights. https://www.kids.org.uk/

Maternal/Parental Mental Health

The Maternal Mental Health Alliance (MMHA) is a UK-wide charity and network of organizations, dedicated to ensuring all women and families impacted by perinatal mental health problems have access to high-quality, compassionate care and support. https://maternal mentalhealthalliance.org/

PANDAS is a UK-based charity offering free perinatal mental illness support services, including a helpline, social media groups, What's App support and e-mail support. https://pandasfoundation.org.uk/

The Samaritans offer a wide range of support services relating to mental health, with a free 24/7 support line. https://www.samaritans.org/

Mind is a UK-based charity making mental health an everyday priority. They offer information and advice on many topics relating to mental health, including mental health and parenting. https://www.mind.org.uk/information-support/tips-for-everyday-living/parenting-and-mental-health/

Adult Trauma after Childhood Abuse

The NSPCC offer services to help children who've been abused, protect children at risk and find the best ways to prevent child abuse from ever happening. https://www.nspcc.org.uk/

INDIA

CHILDLINE 1098 is a phone number that spells hope for millions of children across India. It is a 24 hours a day, 365 days a year, free, emergency phone service for children in need of aid and assistance. CHILDLINE India Foundation (CIF) is the nodal agency of the

Union Ministry of Women and Child Development. https://www.
childlineindia.org/

Sneha is a suicide prevention organization in Chennai, India. Sneha
offers unconditional emotional support to anyone who could be
feeling distressed, depressed or suicidal. No matter what situation you
are in, or what choices you have made in your life; if something is
bothering you, or weighing you down, you can talk to Sneha about it.
https://snehaindia.org/new/

Tele MANAS is a comprehensive mental health care service. You can dial
the Toll-free numbers on the website to get in touch with counselors.
https://telemanas.mohfw.gov.in/#/home

Mpowerminds empower individuals and their families from all walks of
life by creating awareness, fostering education and alleviating stigma
vis-à-vis mental health. They provide holistic care, interventions
and treatments that are world-class and multi-disciplinary, so that
individuals with mental concerns may lead meaningful and productive
lives with the utmost respect and dignity. https://mpowerminds.com/

USA

Better Help is the world's largest therapy service, offering online therapy
for adults, couples and teenagers. Better Helps' mission is making
professional therapy accessible, affordable, and convenient—so
anyone who struggles with life's challenges can get help, anytime and
anywhere. https://www.betterhelp.com

The Psychology Today website offers a resource for finding, reviewing,
and assessing therapists in your area. https://www.psychologytoday.
com/intl

The Trevor Project provide information and support to LGBTQ young
people 24/7, all year round. Through their website, you can reach out
to a counselor, find answers and information, and get the tools you
need to help someone else. https://www.thetrevorproject.org

The 988 Suicide & Crisis Lifeline (formerly known as the National Suicide
Prevention Lifeline) provides free and confidential emotional support
to people in suicidal crisis or emotional distress 24 hours a day, 7

days a week, across the United States. The Lifeline is comprised of a national network of over 200 local crisis centers, combining custom local care and resources with national standards and best practices. https://www.988lifeline.org

ABOUT THE AUTHORS

JAYNE RUFF

Jayne lives in London with her husband and two children. Originally from Scotland, she is an Occupational Psychologist working with global teams through organizational development and change. Jayne is also the founder of coaching and development consultancy—Parenting Point—and she is passionate about supporting people as they navigate working parenthood. Jayne talks openly about her own struggles juggling work and home life and how she uses psychology to feel more confident in her parenting and professional choices. Outside of work, Jayne enjoys nothing more than spending time with her family in the great outdoors.

AARTHI PRABHAKARAN

Aarthi has 20+ years of multi-faceted experience in providing Consulting to EdTech Start-ups, Integrative Counseling & Community Development, impacting new-age entrepreneurs, diverse student and family populations. Her international relocations enriched her expertise to apply global best practices in any local context. Pursuing her passion in Counseling Psychology, she runs an exclusive life skills program—ChangeMakers—for teens and young adults, to inculcate the aspects of problem solving, holistic well-being, and being a learner for life like herself. She is an alumna of BITS Pilani.

ANJNA PARAMESWARAN

Anjna is an English teacher with an immense love for nature, books and animals. Anjna is currently living and learning from Bengaluru, Karnataka after having lived and worked across India.

JAITA MULLICK

Jaita has been in the sphere of Corporate Learning & Development, Mentorship and Planning for over 15 years in India. An avid reader and blogger, she is of late experimenting with newer technologies in building growth strategies in the work environment. She is a social activist, loves adventure, and takes out time for travel, which keeps her and her little one busy exploring Bengaluru, and beyond.

CHANDRIKA IYER

Chandrika is an educator and a certified counselor. She has a combined experience of more than four decades dealing with children and parents. She brings her vast expertise in engaging with children and parents of different cultures and countries to her practice as a parent coach and counselor for children and young adults. Chandrika has a Masters in Curriculum and Teaching from Michigan State University and advanced certification in Rational Emotive Behavior Therapy (REBT) and Cognitive Behavior Therapy (CBT) from the Albert Ellis Institute, New York. In addition, she has continuously upgraded her skill set by getting certifications in Dialectical Behavior Therapy for families and children and in Acceptance and Commitment Therapy (ACT). She is passionate about advocating emotional education as part of the school and college curriculum. She believes that imparting Social and Emotional Learning (SEL) skills is key to achieving children's mental well-being. Chandrika started The Parenting Club in 2013, which offers coaching, workshops, and sessions for parents and children. Chandrika is a proud grandmother of two granddaughters and lives in Bengaluru, India, with her family.

JENNA CLANCEY

Jenna lives in Charleston with her husband and daughter. Born in New Jersey, Jenna has lived all around the northeast until finally settling in South Carolina in 2018. She has gone through many stages of her career—a Mental

Health Specialist, Special Ed Teacher, Fundraising and Special Events, and finally to Business Development and Management for Witten Clancey Partners, their medical physics consulting company. Jenna is excited to continue to bring to the forefront the importance of conversations about parenting and mental health. Outside of work and family, Jenna loves to spend time at the beach or on the water and organizing outings with friends.

YAGYA MAHADEVAN

Yagya is a Technology Project Manager by profession, working with Software, Infrastructure & Project Management for over 23 years. When he is not spending time with family, he is usually working on projects. Originally from India, living in the United States for last 10 years has given him different perspectives on life with a special needs child and how different parts of the world sees, supports and empathizes with them.

DENISE VARUGHESE

Denise is a reader, writer, partner, mother, and friend. She is from Long Island, New York and now lives in Houston, Texas with her husband, three children, and dog, Blue. Denise has 16 years of experience working in K-12 Education and loves facilitating communities where people can connect and grow.

RAMAKRISHNAN RAJAMANI

Krish Rajamani is a curious learner, hard and smart worker, explorer of nature and food, vivid seeker and giver. He has 22 years of professional and varied career experience as a Software Developer, Hedge Fund Business Analyst, Global Co-ordinator, and Finance System Head, supporting programs to transform systems. He is a coach to people truly looking to transform, and a leader of people in support of realizing individual and organizational visions. As a learner of neuro-linguistic programming (NLP) over 7 years, this has helped Krish discover a lot about himself and others in the ecosystem. Krish is grateful of the opportunities he has had to support people transform their lives, their state and help them just move forward. Krish is a strong believer that to be happy, you should support other people to be happy, and the world then becomes a better place to live every day!

PREETHA BHASKAR

Preetha describes herself as a simple, fun-loving person, who worked in the Telecom Sector and as a Head of Order Management and Forecasting in Supply Chain with a UPS manufacturing company for over a decade. In the quest of exploring new avenues, Preetha spread her wings into the marketing division in a FMCG company. An ardent lover of sarees and jewelery making, Preetha eventually turned to entrepreneurship and now runs a small boutique for sarees and handmade jewelry during the weekends. Preetha believes that following her passion for what she loves has made her who she is today.

ANURADHA GUPTA

Anuradha Gupta (Anu) (she/her) is a Certified Ayurvedic Practitioner, Engineer, MBA, Meditator, Writer and 200 hr. Yoga Teacher. She is an Ayurvedic Doctor-in-Training who will graduate in end 2023. She is a Faculty, Content Specialist and AP Mentor at Kerala Ayurveda USA. She lives in California with her husband and is the proud Mom of two beautiful kids and lovely cats. She is a prolific writer who writes about Ayurveda, sustainability and LGBTQIA+ rights for Art of Living and Kerala Ayurveda. She studied "Queering Identities" and is an active LGBTQIA+ advocate. Anu is on the board of her local PFLAG chapter. She was a guest speaker advocating for LGBTQ+ issues at "Desi Moms," "Queer Story Time," her engineering school, BITS, Pilani on "Embracing LGBTQ+ in the Family" and at San Ramon Diversity Coalition. She volunteers for many nonprofits like Art of Living, Project Welcome Home Troops and Free Mom Hugs. Following in the footsteps of many Mama Bears, Anu is a non-denominational Minister who can officiate LGBTQIA+ weddings and was featured by the Universal Life Church. In 2021, on behalf of the Human Rights Campaign, Anu represented the LGBTQIA+ community at the US Senate to advocate for the Equality Act. Anu was on the DEI committee of the National Ayurvedic Medical Association in the United States for a year. In the Ayurvedic field, she is working hard to make the space LGBTQIA+ affirming. Anu hopes to leave the world a kinder, happier, more inclusive and just place.

ARREN WILLIAMS

Arren Williams is a 62 year old mother and grandmother with hundreds of children and adults that call her Miss Arren. Born and raised in California, she has also called Canada and many other states her home. Property Management, Police Officer, Childcare Provider and Business Consultant are a few of her professional titles. Her true passion is developing young minds and freeing them from trauma and limitations. She is also gifted in culinary arts and would impress the most discerning palate. Arren has experienced half a century of trauma, oppression, addiction, neglect, psychological abuse and sexual assault and rape by family members. Through years of healing work, the adoption of self-empowerment and an open-minded approach, she has transcended the rage and guilt. By combining collective knowledge with the wisdom and practices of great minds, she is alchemizing her pain into love. Her hope is for a healed and restored world, one individual at a time, one family at a time. She truly believes that this will change the world.

OUR EARLY BACKERS

A BIG THANK YOU to our early backers,
who believed enough in our book to pre-order a copy,
when it was merely a landing page.

— Co-Authors, *Imperfect Parenting: Honest Stories from Global Parents*

A B Srinivasan
Adriya Dey
Aishwarya Nair
Alison Fahey
Allison Martinelli
Amie Jones
Amy Fox
Amy Gibbons
Amy White
Ananthi Nagarajan
Andrea French
Anirban Dey
Anita Mohan
Anjna Iyer
Anjul Gupta
Ankita Girish
Anne Ruff
Anuradha Gupta
Archana Prabhakaran
Arnab Ganguly
Arpita Chakraborty

Arpitaa Kedarnath
Arren Williams
Arvind
  Parameswaran
Ashfaq Jiwani
Ashley Davis
Ashley Mcclay
Ashley Prine
Atheeswari Rajkumar
Aubrey Nelson
Autumn Balentine
Aviva Sakolsky
Beth Montemurro
Beth Taverna
Bharath Kandasamy
Bharathi Kalluri
Binda Dey
Bindu Mitter
Brittany Brayson
Caroline Brayson
Caroline Koverman

Casey
  Breslow-Glugeth
Chalapathy MS
Chetan Nagendra
Christopher Burke
Cristina Michelassi
David Genova
Debjyoti Banerjee
Deepa Sudarshan
Denise Lechler
Denise Sarkor
Dharmarajan Sankara
  Subrahmanian
Diana Tang
Dijoy Chand Baral
Dileesh Kumar
Dineet Dadu
Divya Keshamoni
Dr. Chhavi Rosha
Eddie Ruff
Elizabeth Shafer

Ellen Fleming Clark
Erica Halverson
Gayatri V
Geeta Nomula
Geeta Sharma
Geneva Marquina
Gita Viswanaathan
Gokulnath C
Gopinath B
Gordon Callum
Gulnar Sahi
Hariharan
    Krishnamurthy
Harriet Sanderson
Hayley Murphy
Heena Jaisingh
Helen Hailemariam
Helene Sperling
Himadri Gupta
Jack Zarin-Rosenfeld
Jaita Mullick
James McFarlane
James Ruff
Jaya Lakshmi
Jayne Ruff
Jayshree Mehta
Jenna Clancey
Jeremy Williams
Jessica Gregorie
Jessica Lee
Jhacole
    LeGrand-Dunn
Jim Fagan
Jitendra Mantri
Joanna Andrews
Judith Liebert
Julia Murray
K S Nagendra

Kara Nadeau
Kartic Vaidyanathan
Katherine Cannella
Katherine Legreid
Kavya K
Kelly Byrne
Kim Maini
Kimberly Underwood
Kristin Spang
Kristina Stoner
Lavanya
    Venkateswaran
Lavanya D
Laxmana Murthy
Lindsay Zegleman
Lisa Imlach
Madhumitha Bharath
Madison Kilduff
Mahalakshmi Kannan
Mahesh Agrawal
Manas Lele
Manoj Thomas
Maria Garner
Maria Maldonado
Mario Nicholas
Marion Pomeranc
Martina Cortesi
Mary Driver
Matthew Sakolsky
Matthew Witten
Maya Weatherton
Meghal Karekar
Mina Dilip
Monika Anil
Monika Mullick
Monique Dotson
NAGESH RAO
Naina Rewal

Nanda Kumar
    Rajendran
Nandakumar KG
Narasingh Sahu
Natalie Lund
Nazlah Taylor
Neeraj Gupta
Nevin Allan
Nichole Harrison
Nicole Arias Iniguez
Niroshan Ganesan
Noelle Ahearn
Nora Bleich
Oliver Ruff
Piyush Joshi
Prabhu Sowmithiran
Preetha Bhaskar
Preethi Ravi Shankar
Pritam Parvatkar
Priti Gajera
Radha Naresh Kumar
Radha Swaminathan
Raghu Rajagopal
Rahul Sharma
Raji Nr
Rakesh Rao
Ramabhadran Anand
    Padmanabha
Ramakrishnan
    Rajamani
Ramamoorthy
    Subramanian
Raman Sharma
Ranjini Kumar
Renchy Thomas
Richard Halverson
Rijin Malayattil
Ritu Dhingra

Rohan Bharath
Ronita Mullick
Ross Callum
Rupmoy Paul
Ruth White
Sadhna Menon
Samora Noguera
Sanjibanee Rout
Sapna Sharma
Sarah Hoffman
Sarah Traylor
Sarayulyer
Senthil Anand
Senthil Letchumana
Shannon Oleksak
Shara Conroy
Sharma Anjali
Shelley Sakolsky
Shreedevi M

Shreyas Shrivastava
Shweta Maheshwari
Simone Frank
Siva Kumar
Srikanth
   Krishnamurthy
Srividhya
   Balasubramanian
Stephanie Juhas
Sujata Sirsat
Sujitha Sankarappan
Sundar Viswanathan
Sunil Nimma
Sunil Singh
Supriyo Dutta
Susan Callum
Susanna Fontenot
Susannah Knox
Swati Jagtap

T E Narasimhan
Tahireh Lal
Tarah Burris
Trisha Craig
Usha Pillai
Vasantha Priya
Vasanthi Prabhakaran
Vasanthi Prabhakaran
Vasuda Raghavendran
Venkat Kalakuntla
Victoria Hogg
Victoria Peluso
Victoria Soriano
Vijayalakshmi Rajesh
Whitney Hanna
Yadunandan Preetha
Yagya Mahadevan